TWO TREATISES OF GOVERNMENT.

TWO
TREATISES
OF
GOVERNMENT.

BY

JOHN LOCKE.

SALUS POPULI SUPREMA LEX ESTO.

A NEW EDITION CORRECTED.

ISBN: 978-93-5128-888-6(PB)

First Published in 1821
Indian Reprint in 2017

Published by

Kalpaz Publications
C-30, Satyawati Nagar,
Delhi – 110052
E-mail: kalpaz@hotmail.com
Website: kalpazpublications.com
Ph.: +91-9212142040

Cataloging in Publication Data—DK
Courtesy: D.K. Agencies (P) Ltd. <docinfo@dkagencies.com>

Locke, John, 1632-1704, **author.**
Two treatises of government / by John Locke.
pages cm
Reprint. New edition corrected: London : Whitmore and Fenn, 1821.
ISBN 9789351288886

1. Filmer, Robert, 1588?-1653. Patriarcha. 2. Political science—Early works to 1800. 3. Liberty. I. Title.

JC153.L63 2017 DDC 320 23

ADVERTISEMENT

To the Present Edition.

Perhaps the Annals of History do not furnish a period, more appropriate for the dissemination of the political opinions of the Immortal Locke, than the present; when Sovereigns and Governmemts, are eagerly waiting, and readily embracing every opportunity to increase their Power ; and when many of the Governed are equally impatient under the wholesome, as well as the more oppressive Laws of those that govern ; to lay before both parties, the real origin of the power of the One, and for what purpose it was granted ; and the just obedience due by the Other ; when those purposes tend to the preservation, and good of society in general.

London, January, 1821-

PREFACE.

HEADER, thou hast here the beginning and end of a discourse concerning government; what fate has otherwise disposed of the papers that should have fdled up the middle, and were more than all the rest, it is not worth while to tell thee. These, which remain, I hope are sufficient to establish the throne of our great restorer, or present King William; to make good his title, in the consent of the people, which being the only one of all lawful governments, he has more fully and clearly, than any prince in Christendom ; and to justify to the world the people of England, whose love of their just and natural rights, with their resolution to preserve them, saved the nation when it was on the very brink of slavery and ruin. If these papers have that evidence, I flatter myself is to be found in them, there will be no great miss of those which are lost, and my reader may be satisfied without them : for 1 imagine, I shall have neither the time, nor inclination to repeat my pains, and till np the wanting part of my answer, by tracing Sir Robert again, through all the windings and obscurities, which are to be met with in the several branches of his wonderful system. The king, and body of the nation, have since so thoroughly confuted his Hypothesis, that I suppose no body hereafter will have either the confidence to appear against our common safety, and be again an advocate for slavery; or the weakness to be deceived with contradictions dressed up in a popular stile, and well-turned periods : for if any one will be at the pains, himself, in those parts, which are here untouched, to strip Sir Robert's discourses of the flourish of doubtful expressions, and endeavour to reduce his words to direct, positive, intelligible propositions, and then compare them one with another, he will quickly be satisfied, there was never so much glib nonsense put together in well-sounding English. If he think it not worth while to examine his works all through, let him make an experiment in that part, where lie treats of usurpation ; and lot him try, whether he can, with all his skill, make Sir Robert intelligible, and consistent with himself, or common sense. J should not speak so plainly of a gentlemen. long since past answering, had not the pulpit, of late years, publicly owned his doctrine, and made it the current divinity of the times. It is necessary those men, who taking on them to be teachers, have so dangerously misled others, should be openly shewed of what authority this their Patriarch is, whom they have so blindly followed, so that they may either retract what upon so ill grounds they have vented, and cannot be maintained ; or else justify those principles which they preached up for gospel ; though they had no better an author than an English courtier: for [should not concerning government: that so at last all times might not have reason to complain of the drum ecclesiastic. If any one, concerned really for truth, undertake the confutation of my hypothesis, I promise him either to recant mistake, upon fair conviction ; or to answer his difficulties. But he must remember two things.

First, That cavilling here and there, at some expression, or little incident of my discourse, is not an answer to my book.

Secondly, That I shall not take railing for arguments, nor think either of these worth my notice: Though 1 shall always look on myself as bound to give satisfaction to any one who shall appear to be conscientiously scrupulous in the point, and shall shew any just grounds for his scruples.

I have nothing more, but to advertise the reader, that Observations stands for Observations on Hobbes, Milton, &c. and that a bare quotation of pages always mean Pages of his Patriarcha. Edit. 1680.

CONTENTS

CHAPTER I.

§. 1. Slavery is so vile and miserable an estate of man, and so directly opposite to the generous temper and courage of our nation; that it is hardly to be conceived, that an *Englishman,* much less a gentleman, should plead for it. And truly I should have taken Sir *Robert Filmer*'s *Patriarcha,* as any other treatise, which would persuade all men, that they are slaves, and ought to be so, for such another exercise of wit, as was his who writ the encomium of *Nero;* rather than for a serious discourse meant in earnest, had not the gravity of the title and epistle, the picture in the front of the book, and the applause that followed it, required me to believe, that the author and publisher were both in earnest. I therefore took it into my hands with all the expectation, and read it through with all the attention due to a treatise that made such a noise at its coming abroad, and cannot but confess my self mightily surprised, that in a book, which was to provide chains for all mankind, I should find nothing but a rope of sand, useful perhaps to such, whose skill and business it is to raise a dust, and would blind the people, the better to mislead them; but in truth not of any force to draw those into bondage, who have their eyes open, and so much sense about them, as to consider, that chains are but an ill wearing, how much care soever hath been taken to file and polish them.

§. 2. If any one think I take too much liberty in speaking so freely of a man, who is the great champion of absolute power, and the idol of those who worship it; I beseech him to make this small allowance for once, to one, who, even after the reading of Sir *Robert*'s book, cannot but think himself, as the laws allow him, a freeman: and I know no fault it is to do so, unless any one better skilled in the fate of it, than I, should have it revealed to him, that this treatise, which has lain dormant so long, was, when it appeared in the world, to carry, by strength of its arguments, all liberty out of it; and that from thenceforth our author's short model was to be the pattern in the mount, and the perfect standard of politics for the future. His system lies in a little compass, it is no more but this,

That all government is absolute monarchy.

And the ground he builds on, is this,

That no man is born free.

§. 3. In this last age a generation of men has sprung up amongst us, that would flatter princes with an opinion, that they have a divine right to absolute power, let the laws by which they are constituted, and are to govern, and the conditions under which they enter upon their authority, be what they will, and their engagements to observe them never so well ratified by solemn oaths and promises. To make way for this doctrine, they have denied mankind a right to natural freedom ; whereby they have not only, as much as in them lies, exposed all subjects to the utmost misery of tyranny and oppression, but have also unsettled the titles, and shaken the thrones of princes : (for they too by these men's system, except only one, are all born slaves, and by divine right are subjects to *Adams* right heir;) as if they had designed to make war upon all government, and subvert the very foundation of human society, to serve their present turn.

§. 4. However we must believe them upon their own bare words, when they tell us, we are all born slaves, and we must continue so, there is no remedy for it ; life and thraldom we entered into together, and can never be quit of the one, till we part with the other. Scripture or reason I am sure do not any where say so, notwithstanding the noise of divine right, as if divine authority hath subjected us to the unlimited will of another. An admirable state of mankind, and that which they have not had wit enough to find out till this b 2 latter age. For, however Sir Robert Filmet seems to condemn the novelty of the contrary opinion, *Pair.* p. 3. yet 1 believe it will be hard for him to find any other age, or country of the world, but this, which has asserted monarchy to be *jure divino*. And he confesses, *Patr*. p. 4. That *Heyivard, Blackwood, Barclay, and others, that have bravely vindicated the right of Icings in most points, never thought of this, but with one consent admitted the natural liberty and equality of mankind.*

§. 5. By whom this doctrine came at first to be broached, and brought in fashion amongst us, and what sad effects it gave rise to, I leave to historians to relate, or to the memory of those, who were contemporaries with *Sibthorp* and *Mantuering*, to recollect. My business at present is only to consider what Sir *Robert Filmer,* who is allowed to have carried this argument farthest, and is supposed to have brought it to perfection, has said in it ; for him every one, who . would be as fashionable as *French* was at court, has learned, and runs away with this short system of politics, viz. *Men are not born free, and therefore could never have the liberty to choose either governors, or forms of government* . Princes have their power absolute, and by divine right ; for slaves could never have a right to compact or consent. *Adam* was an absolute monarch, and so arc all princes ever since.

CHAPTER II

Of Paternal and Regal Power.

§. 6. SIR *Robert Filmer*'s great position is, that *men are not naturally free.* This is the foundation on which his absolute monarchy stands, and from which it erects itself to an height, that its power is above every power, *caput inter nubila,* so high above all earthly and human things, that thought can scarce reach it; that promises and oaths, which tye the infinite Deity, cannot confine it. But if this foundation fails, all his fabric falls with it, and governments must be left again to the old way of being made by contrivance, and the consent of men (Ἀνθρωπίνῃ κτίσις) making use of their reason to unite together into society. To prove this grand position of his, he tells us, p. 12. *Menare born in subjection to their parents,* and therefore cannot be free. And this authority of parents, he calls *royal authority,* p. 12, 14. *Fatherly authority, right of fatherhood,* p. 12, 20. One would have thought he would, in the beginning of such a work as this, on which was to depend the authority of princes, and the obedience of subjects, have told us expresly, what that fatherly authority is, have defined it, though not limited it, because in some other treatises of his he tells us, it is unlimited, and unlimit able*; he should at least have given us such an account of it, that we might have had an entire notion of this *fatherhood,* or *fatherly authority,* whenever it came in our way in his writings: this I expected to have found in the first chapter of his *Patriarcha.* But instead thereof, having, 1. *en passant,* made his obeysance to the *arcana imperii,* p. 5. 2. made his compliment to the *rights and liberties of this, or any other nation,* p. 6. which he is going presently to null and destroy; and, 3. made his leg to those learned men, who did not see so far into the matter as himself, p. 7. he comes to fall on *Bellarmine,* p. 8. and, by a victory over him, establishes his *fatherly authority*

---

* In grants and gifts that have their original from God or nature, as the power of the father hath, no inferior power of man can limit, nor make any law of prescription against them. Observations, 158.
The scripture teaches, that supreme power was originally in the father, without any limitation. Observations, 245.

beyond any question. *Bellarmine* being routed by his own confession, p. 11. the day is clear got, and there is no more need of any forces: for having done that, I observe not that he states the question, or rallies up any arguments to make good his opinion, but rather tells us the story, as he thinks fit, of this strange kind of domineering phantom, called the *fatherhood,* which whoever could catch, presently got empire, and unlimited absolute power. He assures us how this *fatherhood* began in *Adam,* continued its course, and kept the world in order all the time of the *patriarchs* till the flood, got out of the ark with *Noah* and his sons, made and supported all the kings of the earth till the captivity of the *Israelites* in *Egypt,* and then the poor *fatherhood* was under hatches, till *God, by giving the* Israelites *kings, re-established the ancient and prime right of the lineal succession in paternal government.* This is his business from p. 12. to 19. And then obviating an objection, and clearing a difficulty or two with one half reason, p. 23. *to confirm the natural right of regal power,* he ends the first chapter. I hope it is no injury to call an half quotation an half reason; for God says, *Honour thy father and mother;* but our author contents himself with half, leaves out *thymother* quite, as little serviceable to his purpose. But of that more in another place.

§. 7. I do not think our author so little skilled in the way of writing discourses of this nature, nor so careless of the point in hand, that he by over-sight commits the fault, that he himself, in his *Anarchy of a mixed Monarchy,* p. 239. objects to Mr. *Hunton* in these words: *Where first I charge the author, that he hath not given us any definition, or description of monarchy in general; for by the rules of method he should have first defined.* And by the like rule of method Sir *Robert* should have told us, what his *fatherhood* or *fatherly authority* is, before he had told us, in whom it was to be found, and talked so much of it. But perhaps Sir *Robert* found, that this *fatherly authority,* this power of fathers, and of kings, for he makes them both the same, p. 24. would make a very odd and frightful figure, and very disagreeing with what either children imagine of their parents, or subjects of their kings, if he should have given us the whole draught together in that gigantic form, he had painted it in his own fancy; and therefore, like a wary physician, when he would have his patient swallow some harsh or *corrosive liquor,* he mingles it with a large quantity of that which may dilute it; that the scattered parts may go down with less feeling, and cause less aversion.

§. 8. *Let us then endeavour to find what account he gives us of this fatherly authority, as it lies scattered in the several parts of his writings. And first, as it was vested in Adam, he says, Not only Adam, but the succeeding patriarchs, had, by right of fatherhood, royal authority over their children, p. 12. This lordship which Adam by command had over the whole world, and by right descending from him the patriarchs did enjoy, was as large and ample as the absolute dominion of any monarch, which hath been since the creation, p. 13. Dominion of life and death, making war, and concluding peace, p. 13. Adam and the patriarchs had absolute power of life and death, p. 35. Kings, in the right of parents, succeed to the exercise of supreme jurisdiction, p. 19. As kingly power is by the law of God, so it hath no inferior law to limit it; Adam was lord of all, p. 40. The father of a family governs by no other law, than by his own will, p. 78. The superiority of princes is above laws, p. 79. The unlimited jurisdiction of kings is so amply described by Samuel, p. 80. Kings are above the laws, p. 93. And to this purpose see a great deal more which our author delivers in Bodin's words: It is certain, that all laws, privileges, and grants of princes, have no force, but during their life; if they be not ratified by the express consent, or by sufferance of the prince following, especially privileges, Observations, p. 279. The reason why laws have been also made by kings, was this; when kings were either busied with wars, or distracted with public cares, so that every private man could not have access to their persons, to learn their wills and pleasure, then were laws of necessity invented, that so every particular subject might find his prince's pleasure decyphered unto him in the tables of his laws, p. 92. In a monarchy, the king must by necessity be above the laws, p. 100. A perfect kingdom is that, wherein the king rules all things according to his own will, p. 100. Neither common nor statute laws are, or can be, any diminution of that general power, which kings have over their people by right of fatherhood, p. 115. Adam was the father, king, and lord over his family; a son, a subject, and a servant or slave, were one and the same thing at first. The father had power to dispose or sell his children or servants; whence we find, that the first reckoning up of goods in scripture, the man-servant and the maid-servant, are numbred among the possessions and substance of the owner, as other goods were, Observations, Pref. God also hath given to the father a right or liberty, to alien his power over his children to any other; whence we find the sale and gift of children to have much been in use in the beginning of the world, when men had their servants for a possession and an inheritance, as well as other goods; whereupon we find the power of castrating and making eunuchs much in use in old times, Observations,p. 155. Law is nothing else but the will of him that hath the power of the supreme father, Observations, p. 223. It was God's ordinance that the supremacy should be unlimited in Adam, and as large as all the acts of his will; and as in him so in all others that have supreme power, Observations, p. 245.*

§. 9. I have been fain to trouble my reader with these several quotations in our author's own words, that in them might be seen his own description of his *fatherly authority,* as it lies scattered up and down in his writings, which he supposes was first vested in *Adam,* and by right belongs to all princes ever since. This *fatherly authority* then, or *right of fatherhood,* in our author's sense, is a divine unalterable right of sovereignty, whereby a father or a prince hath an absolute, arbitrary, unlimited, and unlimitable power over the lives, liberties, and estates of his children and subjects; so that he may take or alienate their estates, sell, castrate, or use their persons as he pleases, they being all his slaves, and he lord or proprietor of every thing, and his unbounded will their law.

§. 10. Our author having placed such a.mighty power in *Adam,* and upon that supposition sounded all government, and all power of princes, it is reasonable to expect, that he should have proved this with arguments clear and evident, suitable to the weightiness of the cause; that since men had nothing else left them, they might in slavery have such undeniable proofs of its necessity, that their consciences might be convinced, and oblige them to submit peaceably to that absolute dominion, which their governors had a right to exercise over them. Without this, what good could our author do, or pretend to do, by erecting such an unlimited power, but flatter the natural vanity and ambition of men, too apt of itself to grow and encrease with the possession of any power? and by persuading those, who, by the consent of their fellowmen, are advanced to great, but limited, degrees of it, that by that part which is given them, they have a right to all, that was not so; and therefore may do what they please, because they have authority to do more than others, and so tempt them to do what is neither for their own, nor the good of those under their care; whereby great mischiefs cannot but follow.

§. 11. The sovereignty of *Adam,* being that on which, as a sure basis, our author builds his mighty absolute monarchy, I expected, that in his *Patriarcha,* this his main supposition would have been proved, and established with all that evidence of arguments, that such a fundamental tenet required; and that this, on which the great stress of the business depends, would have been made out with reasons sufficient to justify the confidence with which it was assumed. But in all that treatise, I could find very little tending that way; the thing is there so taken for granted, without proof, that I could scarce believe myself, when, upon attentive reading that treatise, I found there so mighty a structure raised upon the bare supposition of this foundation: for it is scarce credible, that in a discourse, where he pretends to confute the *erroneous principle* of man's *natural freedom,* he should do it by a bare supposition of *Adam's authority,* without offering any proof for that authority. Indeed he confidently says, that *Adam had royal authority,* p. 12, and 13. *Absolute lordship and dominion of life and death,* p. 13. *An universal monarchy,* p. 33. *Absolute power of life and death,* p. 35. He is very frequent in such assertions; but, what is strange, in all his whole *Patriarcha* I find not one pretence of a reason to establish this his great foundation of government; not any thing that looks like an argument, but these words: *To confirm this natural right of regal power, we find in the Decalogue, that the law which enjoyns obedience to kings, is delivered in the terms, Honour thy father, as if all power were originally in the father.* And why may I not add as well, that in the *Decalogue,* the law that enjoyns obedience to queens, is delivered in the terms of *Honour thy mother,* as if all power were originally in the mother? The argument, as Sir *Robert* puts it, will hold as well for one as the other: but of this, more in its due place.

§. 12. All that I take notice of here, is, that this is all our author says in this first, or any of the following chapters, to prove the *absolute power of Adam,* which is his great principle: and yet, as if he had there settled it upon sure demonstration, he begins his second chapter with these words, *By conferring these proofs and reasons, drawn from the authority of the scripture.* Where those proofs and reasons for *Adam*'s sovereignty are, bating that of *Honour thy father,* above mentioned, I confess, I cannot find; unless what he says, p. 11. *In these words we have an evident confession,* viz. *of* Bellarmine, *that creation made man prince of his posterity,* must be taken for proofs and reasons drawn from scripture, or for any sort of proof at all: though from thence by a new way of inference, in the words immediately following, he concludes, *the royal authority of Adam* sufficiently settled in him.

§. 13. If he has in that chapter, or any where in the whole treatise, given any other proofs of *Adam's royal authority,* other than by often repeating it, which, among some men, goes for argument, I desire any body for him to shew me the place and page, that I may be convinced of my mistake, and acknowledge my oversight. If no such arguments are to be found, I beseech those men, who have so much cried up this book, to consider, whether they do not give the world cause to suspect, that it is not the force of reason and argument, that makes them for absolute monarchy, but some other by interest, and therefore are resolved to applaud any author, that writes in favour of this doctrine, whether he support it with reason or no. But I hope they do not expect, that rational and indifferent men should be brought over to their opinion, because this their great doctor of it, in a discourse made on purpose, to set up the *absolute monarchical power of Adam,* in opposition to the *natural freedom* of mankind, has said so little to prove it, from whence it is rather naturally to be concluded, that there is little to be said.

§. 14. But that I might omit no care to inform myself in our author's full sense, I consulted his *Observations on Aristotle, Hobbes, &c.* to see whether in disputing with others he made use of any arguments for this his darling tenet of *Adam's sovereignty;* since in his treatise of the *Natural Power of Kings,* he hath been so sparing of them. In his Observations on Mr. *Hobbes*'s *Leviathan,* I think he has put, in short, all those arguments for it together, which in his writings I find him any where to make use of: his words are these: *If God created only* Adam, *and of a piece of him made the woman, and if by generationfrom them two, as parts of them, all mankind be propagated: if also God gave to* Adam *not only the dominion over the woman and the children that should issue from them, but also over all the earth to subdue it, and over all the creatures on it, so that as long as* Adam *lived, no man could claim or enjoy any thing but by donation, assignation or permission from him, I wonder,*

&c. Observations, 165. Here we have the sum of all his arguments, for *Adam's sovereignty* and against *natural freedom,* which I find up and down in his other treatises: and they are these following; *God's creation of Adam,* the *dominion* he gave him *over Eve,* and the *dominion* he had as *father over his children:* all which I shall particularly consider.

CHAPTER III.

Of Adam's Title to Sovereignty by Creation.

§. 15. SIR *Robert,* in his preface to his Observations on *Aristotle*'s politics, tells us, *A natural freedom of mankind cannot be supposed without the denial of the creation of* Adam: but how *Adam*'s being created, which was nothing but his receiving a being immediately from omnipotence and the hand of God, gave *Adam* a *sovereignty* over any thing, I cannot see, nor consequently understand, how a *supposition of natural freedom isa denial of* Adam'*s creation,* and would be glad any body else (since our author did not vouchsafe us the favour) would make it out for him: for I find no difficulty to suppose the *freedom of mankind,* though I have always believed the *creation of Adam.* He was created, or began to exist, by God's immediate power, without the intervention of parents or the pre-existence of any of the same species to beget him, when it pleased God he should; and so did the lion, the king of beasts, before him, by the same creating power of God: and if bare existence by that power, and in that way, will give dominion, without any more ado, our author, by this argument, will make the lion have as good a title to it, as he, and certainly the antienter. No! for *Adam* had his title *by the appointment of God,* says our author in another place. Then bare *creation* gave him not dominion, and one might have *supposed mankind free* without *the denying the creation of Adam,* since it was God's *appointment* made him monarch.

§. 16. But let us see, how he puts his *creation* and this *appointment* together. *By the appointment of God,* says Sir *Robert, as soon as* Adam *was created, he was monarch of the world, though he had no subjects; for though there could not be actual government till there were subjects, yet by the right of nature it was due to* Adam *to be governor of his posterity:though not in act, yet at least in habit,* Adam *was a king from his creation.* I wish he had told us here, what he meant *by God's appointment:* for whatsoever providence orders, or the law of nature directs, or positive revelation declares, may be said to be *by God's appointment:* but I suppose it cannot be meant here in the first sense, *i. e.* by providence; because that would be to say no more, but that *as soon as* Adam *was created* he was *de facto* monarch, because *by right of nature it was due to*

Adam, *to be governor of his posterity.* But he could not *de facto* be by providence constituted the governor of the world, at a time when there was actually no government, no subjects to be governed, which our author here confesses. *Monarch of the world* is also differently used by our author; for sometimes he means by it a proprietor of all the world exclusive of the rest of mankind, and thus he does in the same page of his preface before cited: *Adam,* says he, *being commanded to multiply and people the earth, and to subdue it, and having dominion given him over all creatures, was thereby the monarch of the whole world; none of his posterity had any right to possess any thing but by his grant or permission, or by succession from him.* 2. Let us understand then by *monarch* proprietor *of the world,* and by *appointment* God's actual donation, and revealed positive grant made to *Adam,* i. Gen. 28. as we see Sir *Robert* himself does in this parallel place, and then his argument will stand thus, *by the positive grant of God: as soon as* Adam was *created, he was proprietor of the world, because by the right of nature it was due to* Adam *to be governor of his posterity.* In which way of arguing there are two manifest falsehoods. *First,* It is false, that God made that grant to *Adam,* as soon as he was created, since, tho' it stands in the text immediately after his creation, yet it is plain it could not be spoken to *Adam,* till after *Eve* was made and brought to him: and how then could he be *monarch by appointment as soon as created,* especially since he calls, if I mistake not, that which God says to *Eve,* iii. Gen. 16, *the original grant of government,* which not being till after the fall, when *Adam* was somewhat, at least in time, and very much distant in condition, from his *creation,* I cannot see, how our author can say in this sense, that *by God's appointment, as soon as* Adam *was created, he was monarch of the world. Secondly,* were it true that God's actual donation *appointed* Adam *monarch of the world as soon as he was created,* yet the reason here given for it would not prove it; but it would always be a false inference, that God, by a positive donation, *appointed* Adam *monarch of the world, because by right of nature it was due to* Adam *to be governor of his posterity:* for having given him the right of government by nature, there was no need of a positive donation; at least it will never be a proof of such a donation.

§. 17. On the other side the matter will not be much mended, if we understand *by God's appointment* the law of nature, (though it be a pretty harsh expression for it in this place) and *by monarch of the world,* sovereign ruler of mankind: for then the sentence under consideration must run thus: *By the law of nature, as soon as* Adam *was created he was governor of mankind, for by right of nature it was due to* Adam *to be governor of his posterity*; which amounts to this, he was *governor by right of nature,* because he was *governor by right of nature:* but supposing we should grant, that a man is *by nature governor* of his children, *Adam* could not hereby *be monarch as soon as created:* for this right of nature being founded in his being their father, how *Adam* could have a natural right to be governor, before he was a father, when by being a father only he had that *right,* is, methinks, hard to conceive, unless he will have him to be a father before he was a father, and to have a title before he had it.

§. 18. To this foreseen objection, our author answers very logically, *he was governor in habit, and not in act:* a very pretty way of being a governor without government, a father without children, and a king without subjects. And thus Sir *Robert* was an author before he writ his book; not *in act* it is true, but in *habit;* for when he had once published it, it was due to him *by the right of nature,* to be an author, as much as it was *to Adam to be governor of his children,* when he had begot them: and if to be such a *monarch of the world,* an absolute monarch *in habit, but not in act,* will serve the turn, I should not much envy it to any of Sir *Robert*'s friends, that he thought fit graciously to bestow it upon, though even this of *act* and *habit,* if it signified any thing but our author's skill in distinctions, be not to his purpose in this place. For the question is not here about *Adam*'s actual exercise of government, but actually having a title to be governor. Government, says our author, was *due* to Adam *by the right of nature:* what is this right of nature? A right fathers have over their children by begetting them; *generatione jus acquiritur parentibus in liberos,* says our author out of *Grotius, Observations,* 223. The right then follows the begetting as arising from it; so that, according to this way of reasoning or distinguishing of our author, *Adam,* as soon as he was created, had a title *only in habit, and not in act,* which in plain *English* is, he had actually no title at all.

§. 19. To speak less learnedly, and more intelligibly, one may say of *Adam,* he was in a possibility of being *governor,* since it was possible he might beget children, and thereby acquire that right of nature, be it what it will, to govern them, that accrues from thence: but what connection has this with *Adam's creation,* to make him say, that *as soon as he was created, he was monarch of the world?* for it may be as well said of *Noah,* that as soon as he was born, he was monarch of the world, since he was in possibility (which in our author's sense is enough to make a monarch, *a monarch in habit,)* to outlive all mankind, but his own posterity. What such necessary connection there is betwixt *Adam*'s *creation* and his *right to government,* so that a *natural freedom of mankind cannot be supposed without the denial of the creation of* Adam, I confess for my part I do not see; nor how those words, *by the appointment, &c.* Observations, 254. how ever explained, can be put together, to make any tolerable sense, at least to establish this position, with which they end, *viz. Adam was a king from his creation;* a king, says our author, *not in act, but in habit, i. e.* actually no king at all.

§. 20. I fear I have tired my reader's patience, by dwelling longer on this passage, than the weightiness of any argument in it seems to require: but I have unavoidably been engaged in it by our author's way of writing, who, hudling several suppositions together, and that in doubtful and general terms, makes such a medly and confusion, that it is impossible to shew his mistakes, without examining the several senses wherein his words may be taken, and without seeing how, in any of these various meanings, they will consist together, and have any truth in them: for in this present passage before us, how can any one argue against this position of his, that *Adam was a king from his creation,* unless one examine, whether the words, *from his creation,* be to be taken, as they may, for the time of the commencement of his government, as the foregoing words import, *as soon as he was created he was monarch;* or, for the cause of it, as he says, p. 11. *creation made man prince of his posterity?* how farther can one judge of the truth of his being thus king, till one has examined whether king be to be taken, as the words in the beginning of this passage would persuade, on supposition of his *private dominion,* which was, by God's positive grant, *monarch of the world by appointment;* or *king* on supposition of his *fatherly power* over his off-spring, which was by nature, *due by the right of nature;* whether, I say, king be to be taken in both, or one only of these two senses, or in neither of them, but only this, that creation made him prince, in a way different from both the other? For though this assertion, that *Adam was king from his creation,* be true in no sense, yet it stands here as an evident conclusion drawn from the preceding words, though in truth it be but a bare assertion joined to other assertions of the same kind, which confidently put together in words of undetermined and dubious meaning, look like a sort of arguing, when there is indeed neither proof nor connection: a way very familiar with our author: of which having given the reader a taste here, I shall, as much as the argument will permit me, avoid touching on hereafter; and should not have done it here, were it not to let the world see, how incoherences in matter, and suppositions without proofs put handsomely together in good words and a plausible stile, are apt to pass for strong reason and good sense, till they come to be looked into with attention.

CHAPTER IV.

Of Adam's Title to Sovereignty by Donation, Gen. i. 28.

§. 21. HAVING at last got through the foregoing passage, where we have been so long detained, not by the force of arguments and opposition, but the intricacy of the words, and the doubtfulness of the meaning; let us go on to his next argument, for *Adam*'s sovereignty. Our author tells us in the words of Mr. *Selden,* that *Adam by donation from God,* Gen. i. 28. *was made the general lord of all things, not without such a private dominion to himself, as without his grant did exclude his children. This determination of Mr.* Selden, says our author, *isconsonant to the history of the* Bible, *and natural reason,* Observations, 210. And in his Pref. to his Observations on *Aristotle,* he says thus, *The first government in the world was monarchical in the father of all flesh,* Adam *being commanded to multiply and people the earth, and to subdue it, and having dominion given him over all creatures, was thereby the monarch of the whole world: none of his posterity had any right to possess any thing, but by his grant or permission, or by succession from him: The earth, saith the* Psalmist, *hath he given to the children of men, which shew the title comes from fatherhood.*

§. 22. Before I examine this argument, and the text on which it is founded, it is necessary to desire the reader to observe, that our author, according to his usual method, begins in one sense, and concludes in another; he begins here with *Adam*'s propriety, or *private dominion, by donation;* and his conclusion is, *which shew the title comes from fatherhood.*

§. 23. But let us see the argument. The words of the text are these; *and God blessed them, and God said unto them, be fruitful and multiply, and replenish the earth and subdue it, and have dominion over the fish of the sea, and over the fowl of the air, and over every living thing that moveth upon the earth,* i. Gen. 28. from whence our author concludes, *that* Adam, *having here dominion given him over all creatures, was thereby the monarch of thewhole world:* whereby must be meant, that either this grant of God gave *Adam* property, or as our author calls it, *private dominion* over the earth, and all inferior or irrational creatures, and so consequently that he was thereby *monarch;* or 2dly, that it gave him rule and dominion over all earthly creatures whatsoever, and thereby over his children; and so he was *monarch:* for, as Mr. *Selden* has properly worded it, *Adam was made general lord of all things,* one may very clearly understand him, that he means nothing to be granted to *Adam* here but property, and therefore he says not one word of *Adam*'s *monarchy.* But our author says, *Adam was hereby monarch of the world,* which, properly speaking, signifies sovereign ruler of all the men in the world; and so *Adam,* by this grant, must be constituted such a ruler. If our author means otherwise, he might with much clearness have said, that *Adam was hereby proprietor of the whole world.* But he begs your pardon in that point: clear distinct speaking not serving every where to his purpose, you must not expect it in him, as in Mr. *Selden,* or other such writers.

§. 24. In opposition therefore to our author's doctrine, that *Adam was monarch of the whole world,* founded on this place, I shall shew,

1. That by this grant, i. *Gen.* 28. God gave no immediate power to *Adam* over men, over his children, over those of his own species; and so he was not made ruler, or *monarch,* by this charter.

2. That by this grant God gave him not *private dominion* over the inferior creatures, but right in common with all mankind; so neither was he *monarch,* upon the account of the property here given him.

§. 25. 1. That this donation, i. *Gen.* 28. gave *Adam* no power over men, will appear if we consider the words of it: for since all positive grants convey no more than the express words they are made in will carry, let us see which of them here will comprehend mankind, or *Adam*'s posterity; and those, I imagine, if any, must be these, *every living thing that moveth:* the words in *Hebrew* are, rwftin nvr*ie Bestiam Reptantem,* of which words the scripture itself is the best interpreter: God having created the fishes and fowls the 5*th* day, the beginning of the 6*th,* he creates the irrational inhabitants of the dry land, which, *v.* 24. are described in these words, *let the earth bring forth the living creature after his kind; cattle and creeping things, and beasts of the earth, after his kind, and,* v. 2. *and God made the beasts of the earth after his kind, and cattle after their kind, and every thing that creepeth on the earth after his kind:* here, in the creation of the brute inhabitants of the earth, he first speaks of them all under one general name, of *living creatures,* and then afterwards divides them into three ranks, 1. *Cattle,* or such creatures as were or might be tame, and so be the private possession of particular men; 2. ??? which, *ver.* 24, and 25. in our Bible, is translated beasts, and by the *Septuagint* ????a, *wild beasts,* and is the same word, that here in our text, *ver.* 28. where we have this great charter to *Adam,* is translated *living thing,* and is also the same word used, *Gen.* ix. 2. where this grant is renewed to *Noah,* and there likewise translated *beast.* 3.

The third rank were the creeping animals, which *ver.* 24, and 25. are comprised under the word, ?????, the same that is used here, *ver.* 28. and is translated *moving,* but in the former verses *creeping,* and by the *Septuagint* in all these places, ??pet?, or reptils; from whence it appears, that the words which we translate here in God's donation, *ver.*28. *living creatures moving,* are the same, which in the history of the creation, *ver.* 24, 25. signify two ranks of terrestrial creatures, *viz. wild beasts* and *reptils,* and are so understood by the *Septuagint.*

§. 26. When God had made the irrational animals of the world, divided into three kinds, from the places of their habitation, *viz. fishes of the sea, fowls of the air,* and living creatures of the earth, and these again into *cattle, wild beasts,* and *reptils,* he considers of making man, and the dominion he should have over the terrestrial world, *ver.* 26. and then he reckons up the inhabitants of these three kingdoms, but in the terrestrial leaves out the second rank ??? or wild beasts: but here, *ver.* 28. where he actually exercises this design, and gives him this dominion, the text mentions *the fishes of the sea, and fowls of the air,* and the *terrestrial creatures* in the words that signify the *wild beasts* and *reptils,* though translated *living thing that moveth,* leaving out cattle. In both which places, though the word that signifies *wild beasts* be omitted in one, and that which signifies *cattle* in the other, yet, since God certainly executed in one place, what he declares he designed in the other, we cannot but understand the same in both places, and have here only an account, how the terrestrial irrational animals, which were already created and reckoned up at their creation, in three distinct ranks *of cattle, wild beasts,* and *reptils,* were here, *ver.* 28. actually put under the dominion of man, as they were designed, *ver.* 26. nor do these words contain in them the least appearance of any thing that can be wrested to signify God's giving to one man dominion over another, to *Adam* over his posterity.

§. 27. And this further appears from *Gen.* ix. 2. where God renewing this charter to *Noah* and his sons, he gives them dominion over the *fowls of the air, and the fishes of the sea, and the terrestrial creatures,* expressed by ??? and ???? wild beasts and reptils, the same words that in the text before us, i. *Gen.* 28. are translated *every moving thing, that moveth on the earth,* which by no means can comprehend man, the grant being made to *Noah* and his sons, all the men then living, and not to one part of men over another: which is yet more evident from the very next words, *ver.* 3. where God gives every ??? *every moving thing,* the very words used, *ch.* i. 28. to them for food. By all which it is plain that God's donation to *Adam, ch.* i. 28. and his designation, *ver.* 26. and his grant again to *Noah* and his sons, refer to and contain in them neither more nor less than the works of the creation the 5th day, and the beginning of the 6th, as they are set down from the 20th to 26th *ver.* inclusively of the 1st *ch.* and so comprehend all the species of irrational animals of the *terraqueous globe,* tho' all the words, whereby they are expressed in the history of their creation, are no where used in any of the following grants, but some of them omitted in one, and some in another. From whence I think it is past all doubt, that man cannot be comprehended in this grant, nor any dominion over those of his own species be conveyed to *Adam.* All the terrestrial irrational creatures are enumerated at their creation, *ver.* 25. under the names *beasts of the earth, cattle and creeping things;* but man, being not then created, was not contained under any of those names; and therefore, whether we understand the *Hebrew* words right or no, they cannot be supposed to comprehend man, in the very same history, and the very next verses following, especially since that *Hebrew* word ??? which, if any in this donation to *Adam, ch.* i. 28. must comprehend man, is so plainly used in contradistinction to him, as *Gen.* vi. 20. vii. 14, 21, 23. *Gen.* viii. 17, 19. And if God made all mankind slaves to *Adam* and his heirs by giving *Adam* dominion over *every living thing that moveth on the earth,* ch. i. 28. as our author would have it, methinks Sir *Robert* should have carried his monarchical power one step higher, and satisfied the world, that princes might eat their subjects too, since God gave as full power to *Noah* and his heirs, *ch.* ix. 2. to eat *every living thing that moveth,* as he did to *Adam* to have dominion over them, the *Hebrew* words in both places being the same.

§. 28. *David,* who might be supposed to understand the donation of God in this text, and the right of kings too, as well as our author in his comment on this place, as the learned and judicious *Ainsworth* calls it, in the 8th *Psalm,* finds here no such charter of monarchical power, his words are, *Thou hast made him,* i. e. man, the Son of man, *a little lower than the angels; thou madest him to have dominion over the works of thy hands; thou hast put allthings under his feet, all sheep and oxen, and the beasts of the field, and the fowls of the air, and fish of the sea, and whatsover passeth thro' the paths of the sea.* In which words, if any one can find out, that there is meant any monarchical power of one man over another, but only the dominion of the whole species of mankind, over the inferior species of creatures, he may, for aught I know, deserve to be one of Sir *Robert's monarchs in habit,* for the rareness of the discovery. And by this time, I hope it is evident, that he that gave *dominion over every living thing that moveth on the earth,* gave *Adam* no monarchical power over those of his own species, which will yet appear more fully in the next thing I am to shew.

§. 29. 2. Whatever God gave by the words of this grant, i. *Gen.* 28. it was not to *Adam* in particular, exclusive of all other men: whatever *dominion* he had thereby, it was not a *private dominion,* but a dominion in common with the rest of mankind. That this donation was not made in particular to *Adam,* appears evidently from the words of the text, it being made to more than one; for it was spoken in the plural number, God blessed *them,* and said unto *them,* Have dominion. God says unto *Adam* and *Eve,* Have dominion; *thereby,* says our author, *Adam was monarch of the world:* but the grant being to them, i. e. spoke to *Eve* also, as many interpreters think with reason, that these words were not spoken till *Adam* had his wife, must not she thereby be lady, as well as he lord of the world? If it be said, that *Eve* was subjected to *Adam,* it seems she was not so subjected to him, as to hinder her *dominion* over the creatures, or *property* in them: for shall we say that God ever made a joint grant to two, and one only was to have the benefit of it?

§. 30. But perhaps it will be said, *Eve* was not made till afterward: grant it so, what advantage will our author get by it? The text will be only the more directly against him, and shew that God, in this donation, gave the world to mankind in common, and not to *Adam* in particular. The word *them* in the text must include the species of man, for it is certain *them* can by no means signify *Adam* alone. In the 26th verse, where God declares his intention to give this dominion, it is plain he meant, that he would make a species of creatures, that should have dominion over the other species of this terrestrial globe: the words are, *And God said, Let us make man in our image, after our likeness, and let them have dominion over the fish,* &c. *They* then were to have dominion. Who? even those who were to have the *image* of God, the individuals of that species of *man,* that he was going to make; for that *them* should signify *Adam* singly, exclusive of the rest that should be in the world with him, is against both scripture and all reason: and it cannot possibly be made sense, if *man* in the former part of the *verse* do not signify the same with *them* in the latter; only *man* there, as is usual, is taken for the species, and *them* the individuals of that species: and we have a reason in the very text. God makes him *in his own image, after his own likeness;* makes him an intellectual creature, and so capable of *dominion:* for wherein soever else the *image of God* consisted, the intellectual nature was certainly a part of it, and belonged to the whole species, and enabled them to have *dominion* over the inferior creatures; and therefore *David* says in the 8th *Psalm* above cited, *Thou hast made him little lower than the angels, thou hast made him to have dominion.* It is not of *Adam* king *David* speaks here, for *verse* 4. it is plain, it is of *man, and the son of man,* of the species of mankind.

§. 31. And that this grant spoken to *Adam* was made to him, and the whole species of man, is clear from our author's own proof out of the *Psalmist. The earth,* faith the Psalmist, *hath he given to the children of men; which shews the title comes from fatherhood.* These are Sir *Robert*'s words in the preface before cited, and a strange inference it is he makes; *God hath given the earth to the children of men,* ergo *the title comes from fatherhood.* It is pity the propriety of the *Hebrew* tongue had not used *fathers of men,* instead of *children of men,* to express mankind: then indeed our author might have had the countenance of the sound of the words, to have placed the *title* in the *fatherhood.* But to conclude, that the *fatherhood* had the right to the earth, because God gave it *to the children of men,* is a way of arguing peculiar to our author: and a man must have a great mind to go contrary to the sound as well as sense of the words, before he could light on it. But the sense is yet harder, and more remote from our author's purpose: for as it stands in his preface, it is to prove *Adam*'s being monarch, and his reasoning is thus, *God gave the earth to the children of men,* ergo *Adam was monarch of the world.* I defy any man to make a more pleasant conclusion than this, which cannot be excused from the most obvious absurdity, till it can be shewn, that *by children of men,* he who had no father, *Adam* alone is signified; but whatever our author does, the scripture speaks not nonsense.

§. 32. To maintain this *property and private dominion of* Adam, our author labours in the following page to destroy the community granted to *Noah* and his sons, in that parallel place, ix. *Gen.* 1, 2, 3. and he endeavours to do it two ways.

1. Sir *Robert* would persuade us against the express words of the scripture, that what was here granted to *Noah,* was not granted to his sons in common with him. His words are, *As for the general community between* Noah *and his sons, which Mr.* Selden *will have to be granted to them,* ix. Gen. 2. *the text doth not warrant it.* What *warrant* our author would have, when the plain express words of scripture, not capable of another meaning, will not satisfy him, who pretends to build wholly on scripture, is not easy to imagine. The text says, *God blessed* Noah *and his sons, and said unto them,* i. e. as our author would have it, *unto him: for,* faith he, *although the sons are there mentioned with* Noah *in the blessing, yet it may best be understood, with a subordination or benediction in succession,* Observations, 211. That indeed is *best,* for our author to be understood, which best serves to his purpose; but that truly *may best be understood* by any body else, which best agrees with the plain construction of the words, and arises from the obvious meaning of the place; and then with *subordination* and *in succession,* will not *be best understood,* in a grant of God, where he himself put them not, nor mentions any such limitation. But yet, our author has reasons, why it *may best be understood so. The blessing,* says he in the following words, *might truly be fulfilled, if the sons, either under or after their father, enjoyed a private dominion,* Observations, 211. which is to say, that a grant, whose express words give a joint title in present (for the text says, into your hands they are delivered) *may best be understood with a subordination* or in *succession;* because it is possible, that in *subordination,* or in *succession,* it may be enjoyed. Which is all one as to say, that a grant of any thing in present possession *may best be understood* of reversion; because it is possible one may live to enjoy it in reversion. If the grant be indeed to a father and to his sons after him, who is so kind as to let his children enjoy it presently in common with him, one may truly say, as to the event one will be as good as the other; but it can never be true, that what the express words grant in possession, and in common, *may best be understood,* to be in reversion. The sum of all his reasoning amounts to this: God did not give to the sons of *Noah* the world in common with their father, because it was possible they might enjoy it under, or after him. A very

good sort of argument against an express text of scripture: but God must not be believed, though he speaks it himself, when he says he does any thing, which will not consist with Sir *Robert*'s hypothesis.

§. 33. For it is plain, however he would exclude them, that part of this *benediction,* as he would have it in *succession,* must needs be meant to the sons, and not to *Noah* himself at all: *Be fruitful, and multiply, and replenish the earth,* says God, in this blessing. This part of the benediction, as appears by the sequel, concerned not *Noah* himself at all; for we read not of any children he had after the flood; and in the following chapter, where his posterity is reckoned up, there is no mention of any; and so this *benediction in succession* was not to take place till 350 years after: and to save our author's imaginary *monarchy,* the peopling of the world must be deferred 350 years; for this part of the benediction cannot be understood with *subordination,* unless our author will say, that they must ask leave of their father *Noah* to lie with their wives. But in this one point our author is constant to himself in all his discourses, he takes great care there should be monarchs in the world, but very little that there should be people; and indeed his way of government is not the way to people the world: for how much absolute monarchy helps to fulfil this great and primary blessing of God Almighty, *Be fruitful, and multiply, and replenish the earth,* which contains in it the improvement too of arts and sciences, and the conveniences of life, may be seen in those large and rich countries which are happy under the *Turkish* government, where are not now to be found one third, nay in many, if not most parts of them one thirtieth, perhaps I might say not one hundredth of the people, that were formerly, as will easily appear to any one, who will compare the accounts we have of it at this time, with antient history. But this by the by.

§. 34. The other parts of this *benediction,* or *grant,* are so expressed, that they must needs be understood to belong equally to them all; as much to *Noah*'s sons as to *Noah* himself, and not to his sons *with a subordination,* or *in succession. The fear of you, and the dread of you,* says God, *shall be upon every beast,* &c. Will any body but our author say, that the creatures feared and stood in awe of *Noah* only, and not of his sons without his leave, or till after his death? And the following words, *into your hands they are delivered,* are they to be understood as our author says, if your father please, or they shall be delivered into your hands hereafter? If this be to argue from scripture, I know not what may not be proved by it; and I can scarce see how much this differs from that *fiction and fansie,* or how much a surer foundation it will prove, than the opinions of *philosophers and poets,* which our author so much condemns in his preface.

§. 35. But our author goes on to prove, that *it may best be understood with a subordination, or a benediction in succession; for,* says he, *it is not probable that the private dominion which God gave to* Adam, *and by his donation, assignation, or cession to his children, was abrogated, and a community of all things instituted between* Noah *and his sons*——Noah *was left the sole heir of the world; why should it be thoughtthat God would disinberit him of his birth-right, and make him of all men in the world the only tenant in common with his children?* Observations, 211.

§. 36. The prejudices of our own ill-grounded opinions, however by us called *probable,* cannot authorise us to understand scripture contrary to the direct and plain meaning of the words. I grant, it is not probable, that *Adam*'s *private dominion* was here *abrogated:* because it is more than improbable, (for it will never be proved) that ever *Adam* had any such *private dominion:* and since parallel places of scripture are most probable to make us know how they *may be best understood,* there needs but the comparing this blessing here to *Noah* and his sons after the flood, with that to *Adam* after the creation, i. *Gen.* 28. to assure any one that God gave *Adam* no such *private dominion.* It is *probable,* I confess, that *Noah* should have the same title, the same property and dominion after the flood, that *Adam* had before it: but since *private dominion* cannot consist with the blessing and grant God gave to him and his sons in common, it is a sufficient reason to conclude, that *Adam* had none, especially since in the donation made to him, there are no words that express it, or do in the least favour it; and then let my reader judge whether *it may best be understood,* when in the one place there is not one word for it, not to say what has been above proved, that the text itself proves the contrary; and in the other, the words and sense are directly against it.

§. 37. But our author says, Noah *was the sole heir of the world; why should it be thought that God would disinherit him of his birth-right? Heir,* indeed, in *England,* signifies the eldest son, who is by the law of *England* to have all his father's land; but where God ever appointed any such *heir of the world,* our author would have done well to have shewed us; and how *God disinherited him of his birth-right,* or what harm was done him if God gave his sons a right to make use of a part of the earth for the support of themselves and families, when the whole was not only more than *Noah* himself, but infinitely more than they all could make use of, and the possessions of one could not at all prejudice, or, as to any use, streighten that of the other.

§. 38. Our author probably foreseeing he might not be very successful in persuading people out of their senses, and, say what he could, men would be apt to believe the plain words of scripture, and think, as they saw, that the grant was spoken to *Noah* and his sons jointly; he endeavours to insinuate, as if this grant to *Noah* conveyed no property, no dominion; because, *subduing the earth and dominion over the creatures are therein omitted, nor the earth once named.* And therefore, says he, *there is a considerabledifference between these two texts; the first blessing gave* Adam *a dominion over the earth and all creatures; the latter allows* Noah *liberty to use the living creatures for food: here is no alteration or diminishing of his title to a property of all things, but an enlargement only of his commons,* Observations, 211. So that in our author's sense, all that was said here to *Noah* and his sons, gave them no dominion, no property, but only *enlarged* the *commons; their commons,* I should say, since God says, *to you are they given,* though our author says *his;* for as for *Noah*'s sons, they, it seems, by Sir *Robert*'s appointment, during their father's life-time, were to keep fasting days.

§. 39. Any one but our author would be mightily suspected to be blinded with prejudice, that in all this blessing to *Noah* and his sons, could see nothing but *only* an enlargement of commons: for as to *dominion,* which our author thinks omitted, *the fear of you, and the dread of you,* says God, *shall be upon every beast,* which I suppose expresses the *dominion,* or superiority was designed man over the living creatures, as fully as may be; for in that fear and dread seems chiefly to consist what was given to *Adam* over the inferior animals; who, as absolute a monarch as he was, could not make bold with a lark or rabbet to satisfy his hunger, and had the herbs but in common with the beasts, as is plain from i *Gen.* 2, 9, and 30. In the next place, it is manifest that in this blessing to *Noah* and his sons, property is not only given in clear words, but in a larger extent than it was to *Adam. Into your hands they are given,* says God to *Noah* and his sons; which words, if they give not property, nay, property in possession, it will be hard to find words that can; since there is not a way to express a man's being possessed of any thing more natural, nor more certain, than to say, *it is delivered into his hands.* And *ver.* 3. to shew, that they had then given them the utmost property man is capable of, which is to have a right to destroy any thing by using it; *Every moving thing that liveth,* saith God, *shall be meat for you;* which was not allowed to *Adam* in his charter. This our author calls, *a liberty of using them for food, and only an enlargement of commons, but no alteration of property,* Observations, 211. What other property man can have in the creatures, but the *liberty of using them,* is hard to be understood: so that if the first blessing, as our author says, gave Adam *dominion over the creatures,* and the blessing to *Noah* and his sons, gave them *such a liberty to use them,* as *Adam* had not; it must needs give them something that *Adam* with all his sovereignty wanted, something that one would be apt to take for a greater property; for certainly he has no absolute dominion over even the brutal part of the creatures; and the property he has in them is very narrow and scanty, who cannot make that use of them, which is permitted to another. Should any one who is absolute lord of a country, have bidden our author *subdue the earth,* and given him dominion over the creatures in it, but not have permitted him to have taken a kid or a lamb out of the flock, to satisfy his hunger, I guess, he would scarce have thought himself lord or proprietor of that land, or the cattle on it; but would have found the difference between *having dominion,* which a shepherd may have, and having full property as an owner. So that, had it been his own *case,* Sir *Robert,* I believe, would have thought here was an *alteration,* nay, an enlarging of *property;* and that *Noah* and his children had by this grant, not only property given them, but such a property given them in the creatures, as *Adam* had not: For however, in respect of one another, men may be allowed to have propriety in their distinct portions of the creatures; yet in respect of God the maker of heaven and earth, who is sole lord and proprietor of the whole world, man's propriety in the creatures is nothing but that *liberty to use them,* which God has permitted; and so man's property may be altered and enlarged, as we see it was here, after the flood, when other uses of them are allowed, which before were not. From all which I suppose it is clear, that neither *Adam,* nor *Noah,* had any *private dominion,* any property in the creatures, exclusive of his posterity, as they should successively grow up into need of them, and come to be able to make use of them.

§. 40. Thus we have examined our author's argument for *Adam*'s *monarchy,* founded on the blessing pronounced, i. *Gen.* 28. Wherein I think it is impossible for any sober reader, to find any other but the setting of mankind above the other kinds of creatures, in this habitable earth of ours. It is nothing but the giving to man, the whole species of man, as the chief inhabitant, who is the image of his Maker, the dominion over the other creatures. This lies so obvious in the plain words, that any one, but our author, would have thought it necessary to have shewn, how these words, that seemed to say the quite contrary, gave *Adam monarchical absolute power* over other men, or the *sole property* in all the creatures; and methinks in a business of this moment, and that whereon he builds all that follows, he should have done something more than barely cite words, which apparently make against him; for I confess, I cannot see any thing in them, tending to *Adam's monarchy,* or *private dominion,* but quite the contrary. And I the less deplore the dulness of my apprehension herein, since I find the apostle seems to have as little notion of any such *private dominion of Adam* as I, when he says, God *gives us all things richly to enjoy,* which he could not do, if it were all given away already, to Monarch *Adam,* and the monarchs his heirs and successors. To conclude, this text is so far from proving *Adam* sole proprietor, that, on the contrary, it is a confirmation of the original community of all things amongst the sons of men, which appearing from this donation of God, as well as other places of scripture, the sovereignty of *Adam,* built upon his *private dominion,* must fall, not having any foundation to support it.

§. 41. But yet, if after all, any one will needs have it so, that by this donation of God, *Adam* was made sole proprietor of the whole earth, what will this be to his sovereignty? and how will it appear, that *propriety* in land gives a man power over the life of another? or how will the possession even of the whole earth, give any one a sovereign arbitrary authority over the persons of men? The most specious thing to be said, is, that he that is proprietor of the whole world, may deny all the rest of mankind food, and so at his pleasure starve them, if they will not acknowledge his sovereignty, and obey his will. If this were true, it would be a good argument to prove, that there never was any such *property,* that God never gave any such *private dominion;* since it is more reasonable to think, that God, who bid mankind increase and multiply, should rather himself give them all a right to make use of the food and raiment, and other conveniences of life, the materials whereof he had so plentifully provided for them; than to make them depend upon the will of a man for their subsistence, who should have power to destroy them all when he pleased, and who, being no better than other men, was in succession likelier, by want and the dependence of a scanty fortune, to tie them to hard service, than by liberal allowance of the conveniences of life to promote the great design of God, *increase* and *multiply:* he that doubts this, let him look into the absolute monarchies of the world, and see what becomes of the conveniences of life, and the multitudes of people.

§. 42. But we know God hath not left one man so to the mercy of another, that he may starve him if he please: God the Lord and Father of all has given no one of his children such a property in his peculiar portion of the things of this world, but that he has given his needy brother a right to the surplusage of his goods; so that it cannot justly be denied him, when his pressing wants call for it: and therefore no man could ever have a just power over the life of another by right of property in land or possessions; since it would always be a sin, in any man of estate, to let his brother perish for want of affording him relief out of his plenty. As *justice* gives every man a title to the product of his honest industry, and the fair acquisitions of his ancestors descended to him; so *charity* gives every man a title to so much out of another's plenty, as will keep him from extreme want, where he has no means to subsist otherwise: and a man can no more justly make use of another's necessity, to force him to become his vassal, by with-holding that relief, God requires him to afford to the wants of his brother, than he that has more strength can seize upon a weaker, master him to his obedience, and with a dagger at his throat offer him death or slavery.

§. 43. Should any one make so perverse an use of God's blessings poured on him with a liberal hand; should any one be cruel and uncharitable to that extremity, yet all this would not prove that propriety in land, even in this case, gave any authority over the persons of men, but only that compact might; since the authority of the rich proprietor, and the subjection of the needy beggar, began not from the possession of the Lord, but the confent of the poor man, who preferred being his subject to starving. And the man he thus submits to, can pretend to no more power over him, than he has consented to, upon compact. Upon this ground a man's having his stores filled in a time of scarcity, having money in his pocket, being in a vessel at sea, being able to swim, *&c.* may as well be the foundation of rule and dominion, as being possessor of all the land in the world; any of these being sufficient to enable me to save a man's life, who would perish if such assistance were denied him; and any thing, by this rule, that may be an oocasion of working upon another's necessity, to save his life, or any thing dear to him, at the rate of his freedom, may be made a foundation of sovereignty, as well as property. From all which it is clear, that though God should have given *Adam private dominion,* yet that *private dominion* could give him no *sovereignty;* but we have already sufficiently proved, that God gave him no *private dominion.*

CHAPTER V.

Of Adam's *Title to Sovereignty by the Subjection of* Eve.

§. 44. THE next place of scripture we find our author builds his monarchy of *Adam* on, is iii. *Gen.* 26. *And thy defire shall be to thy husband, and he shall rule over thee. Here we have* (says he) *the original grant of government,* from whence he concludes, in the following part of the page, *Observations,* 244. *That the supreme power is settled in the fatherhood, and limited to one kind of government, that is, to monarchy.* For let his premises be what they will, this is always the conclusion; let *rule,* in any text, be but once named, and presently *absolute monarchy* is by divine right established. If any one will but carefully read our author's own reasoning from these words, *Observations,* 244. and consider, among other things, *the line and posterity of* Adam, as he there brings them in, he will find some difficulty to make sense of what he says; but we will allow this at present to his peculiar way of writing, and consider the force of the text in hand. The words are the curse of God upon the woman, for having been the first and forwardest in the disobedience; and if we will consider the occasion of what God says here to our first parents, that he was denouncing judgment, and declaring his wrath against them both, for their disobedience, we cannot suppose that this was the time, wherein God was granting *Adam* prerogatives and privileges, investing him with dignity and authority, elevating him to dominion and monarchy: for though, as a helper in the temptation, *Eve* was laid below him, and so he had accidentally a superiority over her, for her greater punishment; yet he too had his share in the fall, as well as the sin, and was laid lower, as may be seen in the following verses; and it would be hard to imagine, that God, in the same breath, should make him universal *monarch* over all mankind, and a day-labourer for his life; turn him out of *paradise to till the ground, ver.* 23. and at the same time advance him to a throne, and all the privileges and ease of absolute power.

§. 45.This was not a time, when *Adam* could expect any favours, any grant of privileges, from his offended Maker. If this be *the original grant of government,* as our author tells us, and *Adam* was now made monarch, whatever

Sir *Robert* would have him, it is plain, God made him but a very poor monarch, such an one, as our author himself would have counted it no great privilege to be. God sets him to work for his living, and seems rather to give him a spade into his hand, to subdue the earth, than a sceptre to rule over its inhabitants. *In the sweat of thy face thou shalt eat thy bread,* says God to him, *ver.* 19. This was unavoidable, may it perhaps be answered, because he was yet without subjects, and had nobody to work for him; but afterwards, living as he did above 900 years, he might have people enough, whom he might command, to work for him; no, says God, not only whilst thou art without other help, save thy wife, but as long as thou livest, shalt thou live by thy labour, *In the sweat of thy face, shalt thou eat thy bread, till thou return unto the ground, for out of it wast thou taken, for dust thou art, and unto dust shalt thou return, v.* 19. It will perhaps be answered again in favour of our author, that these words are not spoken personally to *Adam,* but in him, as their representative, to all mankind, this being a curse upon mankind, because of the fall.

§. 46. God, I believe, speaks differently from men, because he speaks with more truth, more certainty: but when he vouchsafes to speak to men, I do not think he speaks differently from them, in crossing the rules of language in use amongst them: this would not be to condescend to their capacities, when he humbles himself to speak to them, but to lose his design in speaking what, thus spoken, they could not understand. And yet thus must we think of God, if the interpretations of scripture, necessary to maintain our author's doctrine, must be received for good: for by the ordinary rules of language, it will be very hard to understand what God says, if what he speaks here, in the singular number, to *Adam,* must be understood to be spoken to all mankind, and what he says in the plural number, i. *Gen.* 26, and 28. must be understood of *Adam* alone, exclusive of all others, and what he says to *Noah* and his sons jointly, must be understood to be meant to *Noah* alone, *Gen.* ix.

§. 47. Farther it is to be noted, that these words here of iii. *Gen.* 16. which our author calls *the original grant of government,* were not spoken to *Adam,* neither indeed was there any grant in them made to *Adam,* but a punishment laid upon *Eve:* and if we will take them as they were directed in particular to her, or in her, as their representative, to all other women, they will at most concern the female sex only, and import no more, but that subjection they should ordinarily be in to their husbands: but there is here no more law to oblige a woman to such a subjection, if the circumstances either of her condition, or contract with her husband, should exempt her from it, than there is, that she should bring forth her children in sorrow and pain, if there could be found a remedy for it, which is also a part of the same curse upon her: for the whole verse runs thus, *Unto the woman he said, I will greatly multiply thy sorrow and thy conception; in sorrow thou shalt bring forth children, and thy desire shall be to thy husband, and he shall rule over thee.* It would, I think, have been a hard matter for any body, but our author, to have found out a grant of *monarchical government to Adam* in these words, which were neither spoke to, nor of him: neither will any one, I suppose, by these words, think the weaker sex, as by a law, so subjected to the curse contained in them, that it is their duty not to endeavour to avoid it. And will any one say, that *Eve,* or any other woman, sinned, if she were brought to bed without those multiplied pains God threatens her here with? or that either of our queens, *Mary* or *Elizabeth,* had they married any of their subjects, had been by this text put into a political subjection to him? or that he thereby should have had *monarchical rule* over her? God, in this text, gives not, that I see, any authority to *Adam* over *Eve,* or to men over their wives, but only foretels what should be the woman's lot, how by his providence he would order it so, that she should be subject to her husband, as we see that generally the laws of mankind and customs of nations have ordered it so; and there is, I grant, a foundation in nature for it.

§. 48. Thus when God says of *Jacob* and *Esau,* that *the elder should serve the younger,* xxv. *Gen.* 23. no body supposes that God hereby made *Jacob* *Esau*'s sovereign, but foretold what should *de facto* come to pass.

But if these words here spoke to *Eve* must needs be understood as a law to bind her and all other women to subjection, it can be no other subjection than what every wife owes her husband; and then if this be the *original grant of government* and the *foundation of monarchical power,* there will be as many monarchs as there are husbands: if therefore these words give any power to *Adam,* it can be only a conjugal power, not political; the power that every husband hath to order the things of private concernment in his family, as proprietor of the goods and land there, and to have his will take place before that of his wife in all things of their common concernment; but not a political power of life and death over her, much less over any body else.

§. 49. This I am sure: if our author will have this text to be a *grant, the original grantof government,* political government, he ought to have proved it by some better arguments than by barely saying, that *thy desire shall be unto thy husband,* was a law whereby *Eve,* and *all that should come of her,* were subjected to the absolute monarchical power of *Adam* and his heirs. *Thy desire shall be to thy husband,* is too doubtful an expression, of whose signification interpreters are not agreed, to build so confidently on, and in a matter of such moment, and so great and general concernment: but our author, according to his way of writing, having once named the text, concludes presently without any more ado, that the meaning is as he would have it. Let the words *rule* and *subject* be but found in the text or margent, and it immediately signifies the duty of a subject to his prince; the relation is changed, and though God says *husband,* Sir *Robert* will have it *king; Adam* has presently *absolute monarchical power* over *Eve,* and not only over *Eve,* but *all that should come of her,* though the scripture says not a word of it, nor our author a word to prove it. But *Adam* must for all that be an absolute monarch, and so down to the end of the chapter. And here I leave my reader to consider, whether my bare saying, without offering any reasons to evince it, that this text gave not *Adam* that *absolute monarchical power,* our author supposes, be not as sufficient to destroy that power, as his bare assertion is to establish it, since the text mentions neither *prince* nor *people,* speaks nothing of *absolute* or *monarchical power,* but the subjection of *Eve* to *Adam,* a wife to her husband. And he that would trace our author so all through, would make a short and sufficient answer to the greatest part of the grounds he proceeds on, and abundantly consute them by barely denying; it being a sufficient answer to assertions without proof, to deny them without giving a reason. And therefore should I have said nothing but barely denied, that by this text *the supreme power was settled and founded by God himself, in the fatherhood, limited to monarchy, and that to* Adam'*s person and heirs,* all which our author notably concludes from these words, as may be seen in the same page, *Observations,* 244. it had been a sufficient answer: should I have desired any sober man only to have read the text, and considered to whom, and on what occasion it was spoken, he would no doubt have wondered how our author found out *monarchical absolute power* in it, had he not had an exceeding good faculty to find it himself, where he could not shew it others. And thus we have examined the two places of scripture, all that I remember our author brings to prove *Adam*'s *sovereignty,* that *supremacy,* which he says, *it was God's ordinance should be unlimited in* Adam, *and as large as all the acts of his will,* Observations, 254. viz. i. *Gen.* 28. and iii. *Gen.* 16. one whereof signifies only the subjection of the inferior ranks of creatures to mankind, and the other the subjection that is due from a wife to her husband, both far enough from that which subjects owe the governors of political societies.

CHAPTER VI.

Of Adam's Title to Sovereignty by Fatherhood.

§. 50. THERE is one thing more, and then I think I have given you all that our author brings for proof of *Adam*'s sovereignty, and that is a supposition of a natural right of dominion over his children, by being their father: and this title of *fatherhood* he is so pleased with, that you will find it brought in almost in every page; particularly he says, *not only* Adam, *but the succeeding patriarchs had by right of fatherhood royal authority over their children,* p. 12. And in the same page, *this subjection of children being the fountain of all regal authority,* &c. This being, as one would think by his so frequent mentioning it, the main basis of all his frame, we may well expect clear and evident reason for it, since he lays it down as a position necessary to his purpose, that *every man that is born is so far from being free, that by his very birth he becomes a subject of him thatbegets him,* Observations, 156. so that *Adam* being the only man created, and all ever since being begotten, no body has been born free. If we ask how *Adam* comes by this power over his children, he tells us here it is by begetting them: and so again, *Observations, 223. this natural dominion of* Adam, says he, *may be proved out of* Grotius *himself, who teacheth, that generatione jus acquiritur parentibus in liberos.* And indeed the act of begetting being that which makes a man a father, his right of a father over his children can naturally arise from nothing else.

§. 51.*Grotius* tells us not here how far this *jus in liberos,* this power of parents over their children extends; but our author, always very clear in the point, assures us, it is *supreme power,* and like that of absolute monarchs over their slaves, absolute power of life and death. He that should demand of him, how, or for what reason it is, that begetting a child gives the father such an absolute power over him, will find him answer nothing: we are to take his word for this, as well as several other things; and by that the laws of nature and the constitutions of government must stand or fall. Had he been an absolute monarch, this way of talking might have suited well enough; *proratione voluntas* might have been of force in his mouth; but in the way of proof or argument is very unbecoming, and will little advantage his plea for absolute monarchy. Sir *Robert* has too much lessened a subject's authority to leave himself the hopes of establishing any thing by his bare saying it; one slave's opinion without proof is not of weight enough to dispose of the liberty and fortunes of all mankind. If all men are not, as I think they are, naturally equal, I am sure all slaves are; and then I may without presumption oppose my single opinion to his; and be confident that my saying, *that begetting of children makes them not slaves to their fathers, as certainly* sets all mankind free, as his affirming the contrary makes them all slaves. But that this position, which is the foundation of all their doctrine, who would have monarchy to be *jure divino,* may have all fair play, let us hear what reasons others give for it, since our author offers none.

§. 52. The argument, I have heard others make use of, to prove that fathers, by begetting them, come by an absolute power over their children, is this; that *fathers have a power over the lives of their children, because they give them life and being,* which is the only proof it is capable of: since there can be no reason, why naturally one man should have any claim or pretence of right over that in another, which was never his, which he bestowed not, but was received from the bounty of another. 1. I answer, that every one who gives another any thing, has not always thereby a right to take it away again. But 2. They who say the *father* gives life to his children, are so dazzled with the thoughts of monarchy, that they do not, as they ought, remember God, who is *the author and giver of life: it is in him alone we live, move, and have our being.* How can he be thought to give life to another, that knows not wherein his own life consists? Philosophers are at a loss about it after their most diligent enquiries; and anatomists, after their whole lives and studies spent in dissections, and diligent examining the bodies of men, confess their ignorance in the structure and use of many parts of man's body, and in that operation wherein life consists in the whole. And doth the rude plough-man, or the more ignorant voluptuary, frame or fashion such an admirable engine as this is, and then put life and sense into it? Can any man say, he formed the parts that are necessary to the life of his child? or can he suppose himself to give the life, and yet not know what subject is fit to receive it, nor what actions or organs are necessary for its reception or preservation?

§. 53. To give life to that which has yet no being, is to frame and make a living creature, fashion the parts, and mould and suit them to their uses, and having proportioned and fitted them together, to put into them a living soul. He that could do this, might indeed have some pretence to destroy his own workmanship. But is there any one so bold, that dares thus far arrogate to himself the incomprehensible works of the almighty? Who alone did at first, and continues still to make a living soul, he alone can breathe in the breath of life. If any one thinks himself an artist at this, let him number up the parts of his child's body which he hath made, tell me their uses and operations, and when the living and rational soul began to inhabit this curious structure, when sense began, and how this engine, which he has framed, thinks and reasons: if he made it, let him, when it is out of order, mend it, at least tell wherein the defects lie. *Shall he that made the eye not see?* says the Psalmist, *Psalm* xciv. 9. See these men's vanities! the structure of that one part is sufficient to convince us of an all-wise contriver, and he has so visible a claim to us as his workmanship, that one of the ordinary appellations of God in scripture is, *God our Maker, and the Lord our Maker.* And therefore though our author, for the magnifying his *fatherhood,* be pleased to say, *Observations,* 159. *That even the power which God himself exerciseth over mankind is by right of fatherhood,* yet this fatherhood is such an one as utterly excludes all pretence of title in earthly parents; for he is *king,* because he is indeed maker of us all, which no parents can pretend to be of their children.

§. 54. But had men skill and power to make their children, it is not so slight a piece of workmanship, that it can be imagined, they could make them without designing it. What father of a thousand, when he begets a child, thinks farther than the satisfying his present appetite? God in his infinite wisdom has put strong defires of copulation into the constitution of men, thereby to continue the race of mankind, which he doth most commonly without the intention, and often against the consent and will of the begetter. And indeed those who desire and design children, are but the occasions of their being, and when they design and wish to beget them, do little more towards their making, than *Deucalion* and his wife in the fable did towards the making of mankind, by throwing pebbles over their heads.

§. 55. But grant that the parents made their children, gave them life and being, and that hence there followed an absolute power. This would give the *father* but a joint dominion with the mother over them: for no body can deny but that the woman hath an equal share, if not the greater, as nourishing the child a long time in her own body out of her own substance: there it is fashioned, and from her it receives the materials and principles of its constitution: and it is so hard to imagine the rational soul should presently inhabit the yet unformed embrio, as soon as the father has done his part in the act of generation, that if it must be supposed to derive any thing from the parents, it must certainly owe most to the mother. But be that as it will, the mother cannot be denied an equal share in begetting of the child, and so the absolute authority of the *father* will not arise from hence. Our author indeed is of another mind; for he says, *We know that God at the creation gave the sovereignty to the man over the woman, as being the nobler and principal agent in generation,* Observations, 172. I remember not this in my Bible; and when the place is brought where God at the *creation* gave the sovereignty to man over the woman, and that for this reason, because *he is the nobler and principal agent in generation,* it will be time enough to consider, and answer it. But it is no new thing for our author to tell us his own fancies for certain and divine truths, tho' there be often a great deal of difference between his and divine revelations; for God in the scripture says, *his father and his mother that begot him.*

§. 56. They who alledge the practice of mankind, for *exposing or selling* their children, as a proof of their power over them, are with Sir *Robert* happy arguers; and cannot but recommend their opinion, by founding it on the most shameful action, and most unnatural murder, human nature is capable of. The dens of lions and nurseries of wolves know no such cruelty as this: these savage inhabitants of the desert obey God and nature in being tender and careful of their off-spring: they will hunt, watch, fight, and almost starve for the preservation of their young; never part with them; never forsake them, till they are able to shift for themselves. And is it the privilege of man alone to act more contrary to nature than the wild and most untamed part of the creation? doth God forbid us under the severest penalty, that of death, to take away the life of any man, a stranger, and upon provocation? and does he permit us to destroy those, he has given us the charge and care of; and by the dictates of nature and reason, as well as his revealed command, requires us to preserve? He has in all the parts of the creation taken a peculiar care to propagate and continue the several species of creatures, and makes the individuals act so strongly to this end, that they sometimes neglect their own private good for it, and seem to forget that general rule, which nature teaches all things, of self-preservation; and the preservation of their young, as the strongest principle in them, over-rules the constitution of their particular natures. Thus we see, when their young stand in need of it, the timorous become valiant, the fierce and savage kind, and the ravenous tender and liberal.

§. 57. But if the example of what hath been done, be the rule of what ought to be, history would have furnished our author with instances of this *absolute fatherly power* in its height and perfection, and he might have shewed us in *Peru,* people that begot children on purpose to fatten and eat them. The story is so remarkable, that I cannot but set it down in the author's words. "In some provinces, *says he,* they were so liquorish after man's flesh, that they would not have the patience to stay till the breath was out of the body, but would suck the blood as it ran from the wounds of the dying man; they had public shambles of man's flesh, and their madness herein was to that degree, that they spared not their own children, which they had begot on strangers taken in war: for they made their captives their mistresses, and choicely nourished the children they had by them, till about thirteen years old they butchered and eat them; and they served the mothers after the same fashion, when they grew past child bearing, and ceased to bring them any more roasters," *Garcilasso de la Vega hist. des Yncas de Peru,* l. i. c. 12.

§. 58. Thus far can the busy mind of man carry him to a brutality below the level of beasts, when he quits his reason, which places him almost equal to angels. Nor can it be otherwise in a creature, whose thoughts are more than the sands, and wider than the ocean, where fancy and passion must needs run him into strange courses, if reason, which is his only star and compass, be not that he steers by. The imagination is always restless, and suggests variety of thoughts, and the will, reason being laid aside, is ready for every extravagant project; and in this state, he that goes farthest out of the way, is thought fittest to lead, and is sure of most followers: and when fashion hath once established what folly or craft began, custom makes it sacred, and it will be thought impudence, or madness, to contradict or question it. He that will impartially survey the nations of the world, will find so much of their religions, governments and manners, brought in and continued amongst them by these means, that he will have but little reverence for the practices which are in use and credit amongst men; and will have reason to think, that the woods and forests, where the irrational untaught inhabitants keep right by following nature, are fitter to give us rules, than cities and palaces, where those that call themselves civil and rational, go out of their way, by the authority of example. If precedents are sufficient to establish a rule in this case, our author might have found in holy writ children sacrificed by their parents, and this amongst the people of God themselves: the *Psalmist* tells us, *Psal.* cvi. 38. *They shed innocent blood, even the blood of their sons and of their daughters, whom they sacrificed unto the idols of Canaan.* But God judged not of this by our author's rule, nor allowed of the authority of practice against his righteous law; but as it follows there, *the land was polluted with blood; therefore was the wrath of the Lord kindled against his people, insomuch that he abborred his own inheritance.* The killing of their children, though it were fashionable, was charged on them as *innocent blood,* and so had in the account of God the guilt of murder, as the offering them to idols had the guilt of idolatry.

§. 59. Be it then, as Sir *Robert* says, that *anciently* it was usual for men *to sell and castrate their children,* Observations, 155. Let it be, that they exposed them; add to it, if you please, for this is still greater power, that they begat them for their tables, to fat and eat them: if this proves a right to do so, we may, by the same argument, justify adultery, incest and sodomy, for there are examples of these too, both ancient and modern; sins, which I suppose have their principal aggravation from this, that they cross the main intention of nature, which willeth the increase of mankind, and the continuation of the species in the highest perfection, and the distinction of families, with the security of the marriage bed, as necessary thereunto.

§. 60. In confirmation of this natural authority of the father, our author brings a lame proof from the positive command of God in scripture: his words are, *To confirm the natural right of regal power, we find in the Decalogue, that the law which enjoins obedience to kings, is delivered in the terms, Honour thy father,* p. 23. *Whereas many confess, that government only in the abstract, is the ordinance of God, they are not able to prove any such ordinance in the scripture, but only in the fatherly power; and therefore we find the commandment, that enjoins obedience to superiors, given in the terms, Honour thy father; so that not only the power and right of government, but the form of the power governing, and the person having the power, are all the ordinances of God. The first father had not only simply power, but power monarchical, as he was father immediately from God,* Observations, 254. To the same purpose, the same law is cited by our author in several other places, and just after the same fashion; that is, *and mother,* as apochryphal words, are always left out; a great argument of our author's ingenuity, and the goodness of his cause, which required in its defender zeal to a degree of warmth, able to warp the sacred rule of the word of God, to make it comply with his present occasion; a way of proceeding not unusual to those, who embrace not truths because reason and revelation offer them, but espouse tenets and parties for ends different from truth, and then resolve at any rate to defend them; and so do with the words and sense of authors, they would fit to their purpose, just as *Procrustes* did with his guests, lop or stretch them, as may best fit them to the size of their notions: and they always prove like those so served, deformed, lame, and useless.

§. 61. For had our author set down this command without garbling, as God gave it, and joined *mother* to father, every reader would have seen, that it had made directly against him; and that it was so far from establishing the *monarchical power of the father,* that it set up the *mother* equal with him, and enjoined nothing but what was due in common, to both father and mother: for that is the constant tenor of the scripture, *Honour thy father and thy mother,* Exod. xx. *He that smiteth his father or mother, shall surely be put to death,* xxi. 15. *He that curseth his father or mother, shall surely be put to death, ver.* 17. Repeated *Lev.* xx. 9. and by our Saviour, *Matth.* xv. 4. *Ye shall fear every man his mother and his father,* Lev. xix. 3. *If a man have a rebellious son, which will not obey the voice of his father, or the voice of his mother; then shall his father and his mother lay hold on him, and say, This our son is stubbornand rebellious, he will not obey our voice,* Deut. xxi. 18, 19, 20, 21. *Cunsed be he that setteth light by his father or his mother,* xxviii. 16. *My son, hear the instructions of thy father, and forsake not the law of thy mother,* are the words of *Solomon,* a king who was not ignorant of what belonged to him as a father or a king; and yet he joins *father* and *mother* together, in all the instructions he gives children quite thro' his book of *Proverbs. Woe unto him, that sayeth unto his father, What begettest thou, or to the woman, What hast thou brought forth?* Isa. xi. ver. 10. *In thee have they set light by father or mother,* Ezek. xxviii. 2. *And it shall come to pass, that when any shall yet prophesy, then his father and his mother that begat him, shall say unto him, Thou shalt not live, and his father and his mother that begat him, shall thrust him through when he prophesieth,* Zech. xiii. 3. Here not the father only, but the father and mother jointly, had power in this case of life and death. Thus ran the law of the Old Testament, and in the New they are likewise joined, in the obedience of their children, *Eph.* vi. 1. The rule is, *Children, obey your parents;* and I do not remember, that I any where read, *Children, obey your father,* and no more: the scripture joins *mother* too in that homage, which is due from children; and had there been any text, where the honour or obedience of children had been directed to the *father* alone, it is not likely that our author, who pretends to build all upon scripture, would have omitted it: nay, the scripture makes the authority of *father and mother,* in respect of those they have begot, so equal, that in some places it neglects even the priority of order, which is thought due to the father, and the *mother* is put first, as *Lev.* xix. 3. from which so constantly joining father and mother together, as is found quite through the scripture, we may conclude that the honour they have a title to from their children, is one common right belonging so equally to them both, that neither can claim it wholly, neither can be excluded.

§. 62. One would wonder then how our author infers from the 5th commandment, that all *power was originally in the father;* how he finds *monarchical power of government settled and fixed by the commandment, Honour thy father and thy mother.* If all the honour due by the commandment, be it what it will, be the only right of the *father,* because he, as our author says, *has the sovereignty over the woman, as being the nobler and principler agent in generation,* why did God afterwards all along join the *mother* with him, to share in his honour? can the father, by this sovereignty of his, discharge the child from paying this honour to his *mother?* The scripture gave no such licence to the *Jews,* and yet there were often breaches wide enough betwixt husband and wife, even to divorce and separation: and, I think, no body will say a child may with-hold honour from his mother, or, as the scripture terms it, *set light by her,* though his father should command him to do so; no more than the mother could dispense with him for neglecting to *honour* his father: whereby it is plain, that this command of God gives the father no sovereignty, no supremacy.

§. 63. I agree with our author that the title to this *honour* is vested in the parents by nature, and is a right which accrues to them by their having begotten their children, and God by many positive declarations has confirmed it to them: I also allow our author's rule, *that in grants and gifts, that have their original from God and nature, as the power of the father,* (let me add *and mother,* for whom God hath joined together, let no man put asunder) *no inferior power of men can limit, nor make any law of prescription against them,* Observations, 158. so that the mother having, by this law of God, a right to honour from her children, which is not subject to the will of her husband, we see this *absolute monarchical power of the father* can neither be founded on it, nor consist with it; and he has a power very far from *monarchical,* very far from that absoluteness our author contends for, when another has over his subjects the same power he hath, and by the same title: and therefore he cannot forbear saying himself that *he cannot see how any man's children can be free from subjection to their parents,* p. 12. which, in common speech, I think, signifies *mother* as well as *father,* or if *parents* here signifies only *father,* it is the first time I ever yet knew it to do so, and by such an use of words one may say any thing.

§. 64. By our author's doctrine, the father having absolute jurisdiction over his children, has also the same over their issue; and the consequence is good, were it true, that the father had such a power: and yet I ask our author whether the grandfather, by his sovereignty, could discharge the grandchild from paying to his father the honour due to him by the 5th commandment. If the grandfather hath, by *right of fatherhood,* sole sovereign power in him, and that obedience which is due to the supreme magistrate, be commanded in these words, *Honour thy father,* it is certain the grandfather might dispense with the grandson's honouring his father, which since it is evident in common sense he cannot, it follows from hence, that *Honour thy father and mother,* cannot mean an absolute subjection to a sovereign power, but something else. The right therefore which parents have by nature, and which is confirmed to them by the 5th commandment, cannot be that political dominion, which our author would derive from it: for that being in every civil society supreme somewhere, can discharge any subject from any political obedience to any one of his fellow subjects. But what law of the magistrate can give a child liberty, not to *honour his father and mother?* It is an eternal law, annexed purely to the relation of parents and children, and so contains nothing of the magistrate's power in it, nor is subjected to it.

§. 65. Our author says, *God hath given to a father a right or liberty to alien his power over his children to any other,* Observations, 155. I doubt whether he can *alien* wholly the right of *honour* that is due from them: but be that as it will, this I am sure, he cannot *alien,* and retain the same power. If therefore the magistrate's sovereignty be, as our author would have it, *nothing but the authority of a supreme father,* p. 23. it is unavoidable, that if the magistrate hath all this paternal right, as he must have if *fatherhood* be the fountain of all authority; then the subjects, though fathers, can have no power over their children, no right to honour from them: for it cannot be all in another's hands, and a part remain with the parents. So that, according to our author's own doctrine, *Honour thy father and mother* cannot possibly be understood of political subjection and obedience; since the laws both in the Old and New Testament, that commanded children to *honour and obey their parents,* were given to such, whose fathers were under civil government, and fellow subjects with them in political societies; and to have bid them *honour and obey their parents,* in our author's sense, had been to bid them be subjects to those who had no title to it; the right to obedience from subjects, being all vested in another; and instead of teaching obedience, this had been to foment sedition, by setting up powers that were not. If therefore this command, *Honour thy father and mother,* concern political dominion, it directly overthrows our author's monarchy; since it being to be paid by every child to his father, even in society, every father must necessarily have political dominion, and there will be as many sovereigns as there are fathers: besides that the mother too hath her title, which destroys the sovereignty of one supreme monarch. But if *Honour thy father and mother* mean something distinct from political power, as necessarily it must, it is besides our author's business, and serves nothing to his purpose.

§. 66. *The law that enjoins obedience to kings is delivered,* says our author, *in the terms, Honour thy father, as if all power were originally in the father,* Observations, 254: and that law is also delivered, say I, in the terms, *Honour thy mother,* as if all power were originally in the mother. I appeal whether the argument be not as good on one side as the other, *father and mother* being joined all along in the Old and New Testament where-ever honour or obedience is injoined children. Again our author tells us, Observations, 254. *that this command, Honour thy father, gives the right to govern, and makes the form of government monarchical.* To which I answer, that if by *Honour thy father* be meant obedience to the political power of the magistrate, it concerns not any duty we owe to our natural fathers, who are subjects; because they, by our author's doctrine, are divested of all that power, it being placed wholly in the prince, and so being equally subjects and slaves with their children, can have no right, by that title, to any such *honour or obedience,* as contains in it political subjection: if *Honour thy father and mother* signifies the duty we owe our natural parents, as by our Saviour's interpretation, *Matth.* xv. 4. and all the other mentioned places, it is plain it does, then it cannot concern political obedience, but a duty that is owing to persons, who have no title to sovereignty, nor any political authority as magistrates over subjects. For the person of a private father, and a title to obedience, due to the supreme magistrate, are things inconsistent; and therefore this command, which must necessarily comprehend the persons of our natural fathers, must mean a duty we owe them distinct from our obedience to the magistrate, and from which the most absolute power of princes cannot absolve us. What this duty is, we shall in its due place examine.

§. 67. And thus we have at last got thro' all, that in our author looks like an argument for that *absolute unlimited sovereignty* described, sect. 8. which he supposes in *Adam;* so that mankind ever since have been all born *slaves,* without any title to freedom. But if *creation,* which gave nothing but a being, made not *Adam prince of his posterity:* if *Adam, Gen.* i. 28. was not constituted lord of mankind, nor had a *private dominion* given him exclusive of his children, but only a right and power over the earth, and inferiour creatures in common with the children of men; if also *Gen.* iii. 16. God gave not any political power to *Adam* over his wife and children, but only subjected *Eve* to *Adam,* as a punishment, or foretold the subjection of the weaker sex, in the ordering the common concernments of their families, but gave not thereby to *Adam,* as to the husband, power of life and death, which necessarily belongs to the magistrate: if fathers by begetting their children acquire no such power ove them; and if the command, *Honour thy father and mother,* give it not, but only enjoins a duty owing to parents equally, whether subjects or not, and to the *mother* as well as the *father;* if all this be so, as I think, by what has been said, is very evident; then man has a *natural freedom,* notwithstanding all our author confidently says to the contrary; since all that share in the same common nature, faculties and powers, are in nature equal, and ought to partake in the same common rights and privileges, till the manifest appointment of God, who is *Lord over all, blessed for ever,* can be produced to shew any particular person's supremacy; or a man's own consent subjects him to a superiour. This is so plain, that our author confesses, that Sir *John Hayward, Blackwood* and *Barclay, the great vindicators of the right of kings,* could not deny it, *but admit with one consent the natural liberty and equality of mankind,* for a truth unquestionable. And our author hath been so far from producing any thing, that may make good his great position, *that Adam was absolute monarch,* and so *men are not naturally free,* that even his own proofs make against him; so that to use his own way of arguing, *the first erroneous principle failing, the whole fabric of this vast engine of* absolute power *and* tyranny *drops down of itself,* and there needs no more to be said in answer to all that he builds upon so false and frail a foundation.

§. 68. But to save others the pains, were there any need, he is not sparing himself to shew, by his own contradictions, the weakness of his own doctrine. *Adam*'s absolute and sole dominion is that, which he is every where full of, and all along builds on, and yet he tells us, p. 12. *that as* Adam *was lard of his children, so his children under him had a command and power over their own children.* The unlimited and undivided sovereignty of *Adam*'s *fatherhood,* by our author's computation, stood but a little while, only during the first generation, but as soon as he had grand-children, Sir *Robert* could give but a very ill account of it. *Adam, as father of his children,* faith he, *hath an absolute, unlimited royal power over them, and by virtue thereof over those that they begot, and so to all generations;* and yet *his children,* viz. *Cain* and *Seth,* have a paternal power over their children at the same time; so that they are at the same time *absolute lords,* and yet *vassals* and *slaves; Adam* has all the authority, as *grand-father of the people,* and they have a part of it as fathers of a part of them: he is absolute over them and their posterity, by having begotten them, and yet they are absolute over their children by the same title. *No,* says our author, *Adam's children under him had power over their own children, but still with subordination to the first parent.* A good distinction that sounds well, and it is pity it signifies nothing, nor can be reconciled with our author's words. I readily grant, that supposing *Adam*'s *absolute power* over his posterity, any of his children might have from him a delegated, and so a *subordinate* power over a part, or all the rest: but that cannot be the power our author speaks of here; it is not a power by grant and commission, but the natural paternal power he supposes a father to have over his children. For 1. he says, *As* Adam *was lord of his children, so his children under him had a power over their own children:* they were then lords over their own children after the same manner, and by the same title, that *Adam* was, *i. e.* by right of generation, by right of *fatherhood.* 2. It is plain he means the natural power of fathers, because he limits it to be only *over their own children;* a delegated power has no such limitation, as only over their own children, it might be over others, as well as their own children. 3. If it were a delegated power, it must appear in scripture; but there is no ground in scripture to affirm, that *Adam*'s children had any other power over theirs, than what they naturally had as fathers.

§. 69. But that he means here paternal power, and no other, is past doubt, from the inference he makes in these words immediately following, *I see not then how the children of* Adam, *or of any man else, can be free from subjection to their parents.* Whereby it appears that the *power* on one side, and the *subjection* on the other, our author here speaks of, is that *natural power* and *subjection* between parents and children: for that which every man's children owed, could be no other; and that our author always affirms to be absolute and unlimited. This natural *power* of parents over their children, *Adam* had over his posterity, says our author; and this *power* of parents over their children, his children had over theirs in his life-time, says our author also; so that *Adam,* by a natural right of father, had an absolute unlimited power over all his posterity, and at the same time his children had by the same right absolute unlimited power over theirs. Here then are two absolute unlimited powers existing together, which I would have any body reconcile one to another, or to common sense. For the *salvo* he has put in of *subordination,* makes it more absurd: to have one *absolute, unlimited,* nay *unlimitable power* in subordination to another, is so manifest a contradiction, that nothing can be more. Adam *is absolute prince with the unlimited authority of fatherhood over all his posterity;* all his posterity are then absolutely his subjects; and, as our author says, his slaves, children, and grand-children, are equally in this state of subjection and slavery; and yet, says our author, *the children of* Adam *have paternal,* i. e. *absolute unlimited power over their own children:* Which in plain *English* is, they are slaves and absolute princes at the same time, and in the same government; and one part of the subjects have an absolute unlimited power over the other by the natural right of parentage.

§. 70. If any one will suppose, in favour of our author, that he here meant, that parents, who are in subjection themselves to the absolute authority of their father, have yet some power over their children; I confess he is something nearer the truth: but he will not at all hereby help our author: for he no where speaking of the paternal power, but as an absolute unlimited authority, cannot be supposed to understand any thing else here, unless he himself had limited it, and shewed how far it reached. And that he means here paternal authority in that large extent, is plain from the immediate following words; *This subjection of children being,* says he, *the foundation of all regal authority,* p. 12. *the subjection* then that in the former line, he says, *every man is in to his parents,* and consequently what *Adam*'s grand-children were in to their parents, was that which was the fountain of all *regal authority,* i. e. according to our author, *absolute unlimitable authority.* And thus *Adam*'s children had *regal authority* over their children, whilst they themselves were subjects to their father, and fellow-subjects with their children. But let him mean as he pleases, it is plain he allows *Adam's children to have paternal power,* p. 12. as also all other fathers to have *paternal powerover their children,* Observations, 156. From whence one of these two things will necessarily follow, that either *Adam*'s children, even in his life-time, had, and so all other fathers have, as he phrases it, p. 12. *by right of fatherhood, royal authority over their children,* or else, that *Adam, by right of fatherhood, had not royal authority.* For it cannot be but that *paternal power* does, or does not, give *royal authority* to them that have it: if it does not, then *Adam* could not be sovereign by this title, nor any body else; and then there is an end of all our author's politics at once: if it does give *royal authority,* then every one that has *paternal power* has *royal authority;* and then, by our author's patriarchal government, there will be as many kings as there are fathers.

§. 71. And thus what a monarchy he hath set up, let him and his disciples consider. Princes certainly will have great reason to thank him for these new politics, which set up as many absolute kings in every country as there are fathers of children. And yet who can blame our author for it, it lying unavoidably in the way of one discoursing upon our author's principles? For having placed an *absolute power* in *fathers by right of begetting,* he could not easily resolve how much of this power belonged to a son over the children he had begotten; and so it fell out to be a very hard matter to give all the power, as he does, to *Adam,* and yet allow a part in his life-time to his children, when they were parents, and which he knew not well how to deny them. This makes him so doubtful in his expressions, and so uncertain where to place this absolute natural power, which he calls *fatherhood.* Sometimes *Adam* alone has it all, as p. 13. *Observations,* 244, 245. *& Pref.*

Sometimes *parents* have it, which word scarce signifies the father alone, p. 12, 19.

Sometimes *children* during their fathers life-time, as p. 12.

Sometimes *fathers* of *families,* as p. 78, and 79.

Sometimes *fathers* indefinitely, *Observations,* 155.

Sometimes *the heir to Adam,* Observations, 253.

Sometimes *the posterity of Adam,* 244, 246.

Sometimes *prime fathers, all sons or grand-children of* Noah, *Observations,* 244.

Sometimes the *eldest parents,* p. 12.

Sometimes all *kings,* p. 19.

Sometimes all that have supreme power, *Observations,* 245.

Sometimes *heirs to those first progenitors, who were at first the natural parents of the whole people,* p. 19.

Sometimes an elective king, p. 23.

Sometimes those, whether a few or a multitude, that govern the *common-wealth,* p. 23.

Sometimes he that can catch it, an *usurper,* p. 23. Observations, 155.

§. 72. Thus this *new nothing,* that is to carry with it all power, authority, and government; *this fatherhood,* which is to design the person, and establish the throne of monarchs, whom the people are to obey, may, according to Sir *Robert,* come into any hands, any how, and so by his politics give to democracy royal authority, and make an usurper a lawful prince. And if it will do all these fine feats, much good do our author and all his followers with their omnipotent *fatherhood,* which can serve for nothing but to unsettle and destroy all the lawful governments in the world, and to establish in their room disorder, tyranny, and usurpation.

CHAPTER VII.

Of Fatherhood and Property considered together as Fountains of Sovereignty.

§. 73. In the foregoing chapters we have seen what *Adam*'s monarchy was, in our author's opinion, and upon what titles he founded it. The foundations which he lays the chief stress on, as those from which he thinks he may best derive monarchical power to future princes, are two, *viz. Fatherhoodand property:* and therefore the way he proposes to *remove the absurdities and inconveniencies of the doctrine of natural freedom,* is, *to maintain the natural and private dominion of* Adam, *Observations,* 222. Conformable hereunto, he tells us, the *grounds and principles of government necessarily depend upon the original of property,* Observations, 108. *The subjection of children to their parents is the fountain of all regal authority,* p. 12. *And all power on earth is either derived or usurped from the fatherly power, there being no other original to be found of any power whatsoever,* Observations, 158. I will not stand here to examine how it can be said without a contradiction, that the *first grounds and principles of government necessarily depend upon the original of property,* and yet, *that there is no other original of any power whatsoever, but that of the father:* it being hard to understand how there can be *no other original* but *fatherhood,* and yet that the *grounds and principles of government depend upon the original of property; property and fatherhood* being as far different as lord of a manor and father of children. Nor do I see how they will either of them agree with what our author says, *Observations,* 244. of God's sentence against *Eve,* Gen. iii. 16. *That it is the original grant of government:* so that if that were the *original,* government had not its *original,* by our author's own confession, either from *property* or *fatherhood;* and this text, which he brings as a proof of *Adam*'s power over *Eve,* necessarily contradicts what he says of the *fatherhood,* that it is the *sole fountain of all power:* for if *Adam* had any such regal power over *Eve,* as our author contends for, it must be by some other title than that of begetting.

§. 74. But I leave him to reconcile these contradictions, as well as many others, which may plentifully be found in him by any one, who will but read him with a little attention; and shall come now to consider, how these two originals of government, *Adam's natural and private dominion,* will consist, and serve to make out and establish the titles of succeeding monarchs, who, as our author obliges them, must all derive their power from these *fountains*. Let us then suppose *Adam* made, *by God's donation,* lord and sole proprietor of the whole earth, in as large and ample a manner as Sir *Robert* could wish; let us suppose him also, *by right of fatherhood,* absolute ruler over his children with an unlimited supremacy; I ask then, upon *Adam*'s death what becomes of both his *natural* and *private dominion*? and I doubt not it will be answered, that they descended to his next heir, as our author tells us in several places. But this way, it is plain, cannot possibly convey both his *natural* and *private dominion* to the same person: for should we allow, that all the property, all the estate of the father, ought to descend to the eldest son, (which will need some proof to establish it) and so he has by that title all the *private dominion* of the father, yet the father's *natural dominion,* the paternal power cannot descend to him by inheritance: for it being a right that accrues to a man only by begetting, no man can have this natural dominion over any one he does not *beget;* unless it can be supposed, that a man can have a right to any thing, without doing that upon which that right is solely founded: for if a father by *begetting,* and no other title, has *natural dominion* over his children, he that does not beget them cannot have this *natural dominion* over them; and therefore be it true or false, that our author says, *Observations,* 156. That *every man that is born, by his very birth becomes a subject to him that begets him,* this necessarily follows, *viz.* That a man by his birth cannot become a subject to his brother, who did not beget him; unless it can be supposed that a man by the very same title can come to be under the *natural and absolute dominion* of two different men at once; or it be sense to say, that a man by birth is under the *natural dominion* of his father, only because he begat him, and a man by birth also is under the *natural dominion* of his eldest brother, though he did not beget him.

§. 75. If then the *private dominion of Adam,* i. e. his property in the creatures, descended at his death all entirely to his eldest son, his heir; (for, if it did not, there is presently an end of all Sir *Robert*'s monarchy) and his *natural dominion,* the dominion a father has over his children by begetting them, belonged immediately, upon *Adam*'s decease, equally to all his sons who had children, by the same title their father had it, the sovereignty founded upon *property,* and the sovereignty founded upon *fatherhood,* come to be divided; since *Cain,* as heir, had that of *property* alone; *Seth,* and the other sons, that of *fatherhood* equally with him. This is the best can be made of our author's doctrine, and of the two titles of sovereignty he sets up in *Adam:* one of them will either signify nothing; or, if they both must stand, they can serve only to confound the rights of princes, and disorder government in his posterity: for by building upon two titles to dominion, which cannot descend together, and which he allows may be separated, (for he yields that *Adam's children had their distinct territories by right of private dominion,* Observations, 210.p.40.) he makes it perpetually a doubt upon his principles where the sovereignty is, or to whom we owe our obedience, since *fatherhood* and *property* are distinct titles, and began presently upon *Adam*'s death to be in distinct persons. And which then was to give way to the other?

§. 76. Let us take the account of it, as he himself gives it us. He tells us out of *Grotius,* That *Adam's children by donation, assignation, or some kind of cession before he was dead, had their distinct territories by right of private dominion;* Abel *had his flocks and pastures for them:* Cain *had his fields for corn, and the land of* Nod, *where he built him a city,* Observations, 210. Here it is obvious to demand, which of these two after *Adam*'s death was sovereign? *Cain,* says our author, p. 19. By what title? *As heir; for heirs to progenitors, who were natural parents of their people, are not only lords of their own children, but also of their brethren,* says our author, p. 19. What was *Cain* heir to? Not the entire possessions, not all that which *Adam* had *private dominion* in; for our author allows that *Abel,* by a title derived from his father, had *his distinct territory for pasture by right of private dominion.* What then *Abel* had by *private dominion,* was exempt from *Cain*'s dominion: for he could not have *private dominion* over that which was under the *private dominion* of another; and therefore his sovereignty over his brother is gone with this *private dominion,* and so there are presently two sovereigns, and his imaginary title of *fatherhood* is out of doors, and *Cain* is no prince over his brother: or else, if *Cain* retain his sovereignty over *Abel,* notwithstanding his *private dominion,* it will follow, that the *first grounds and principles of government* have nothing to do with *property,* whatever our author says to the contrary. It is true, *Abel* did not outlive his father *Adam;* but that makes nothing to the argument, which will hold good against Sir *Robert* in *Abel*'s issue, or in *Seth,* or any of the posterity of *Adam,* not descended from *Cain.*

§. 77. The same inconvenience he runs into about *the three sons of Noah,* who, as he says, p. 13. *had the whole world divided amongst them by their father.* I ask then, in which of the three shall we find *the establishment of regal power* after *Noah*'s death? If in all three, as our author there seems to say; then it will follow, that regal power is founded in property of land, and follows *private dominion,* and not in *paternal power,* or *natural dominion;* and so there is an end of paternal power as the fountain of regal authority, and the so-much-magnified *fatherhood* quite vanishes. If the regal power descended to *Shem* as eldest, and heir to his father, then *Noah's division of the world by lot to his sons, or his ten years sailing about the Mediterranean to appoint each son his part,* which our author tells of, p. 15. was labour lost; his division of the world to them, was to ill, or to no purpose: for his grant to *Cham* and *Japhet* was little worth, if *Shem,* notwithstanding this grant, as soon as *Noah* was dead, was to be lord over them. Or, if this grant of *private dominion* to them, over their assigned territories, were good, here were set up two distinct sorts of power, not subordinate one to the other, with all those inconveniences which he musters up against the *power of the people,* Observations, 158. which I shall set down in his own words, only changing *property* for *people. All power on earth is either derived or usurped from the fatherly power, there being no other original to be found of any power whatsoever: for if there should be granted two sorts of power, without any subordination of one to the other, they would be in perpetual strife which should be supreme, for two supremes cannot agree: if the fatherly power be supreme, then the power grounded on private dominion must be subordinate, and depend on it; and if the power* grounded on property *be supreme, then the fatherly power must submit to it, and cannot be exercised without the licence of the proprietors, which must quite destroy the frame and course of nature.* This is his own arguing against two distinct independent powers, which I have set down in his own words, only putting power rising from property, for *power of the people;* and when he has answered what he himself has urged here against two distinct powers, we shall be better able to see how, with any tolerable sense, he can derive all regal authority *from the natural and private dominion of* Adam, from *fatherhood* and *property* together, which are distinct titles, that do not always meet in the same person; and it is plain, by his own confession, presently separated as soon both as *Adam*'s and *Noah*'s death made way for succession: though our author frequently in his writings jumbles them together, and omits not to make use of either, where he thinks it will sound best to his purpose. But the absurdities of this will more fully appear in the next chapter, where we shall examine the ways of conveyance of the sovereignty of *Adam,* to princes that were to reign after him.

CHAPTER VIII.

Of the Conveyance of Adam's sovereign Monarchical Power.

§. 78. SIR *Robert,* having not been very happy in any proof he brings for the sovereignty of *Adam,* is not much more fortunate in conveying it to future princes, who, if his politics be true, must all derive their titles from that first monarch. The ways he has assigned, as they lie scattered up and down in his writings, I will set down in his own words: in his preface he tells us, That *Adam being monarch of the whole world, none of his posterity had any right to possess any thing, but by his grant or permission, or by succession from him.* Here he makes two ways of conveyance of any thing *Adam* stood possessed of; and those are *grants* or *succession.* Again he says, *All kings either are, or are tobe reputed, the next heirs to those first progenitors, who were at first the natural parents of the whole people,* p. 19. *There cannot be any multitude of men whatsoever, but that in it, considered by itself, there is one man amongst them, that in nature hath a right to be the king of all the rest, as being the next heir to* Adam, *Observations,* 253. Here in these places *inheritance* is the only way he allows of conveying monarchical power to princes. In other places he tells us, *Observations,* 155. *All power on earth is either derived or usurped from the fatherly power,* Observations, 158. *All kings that now are, or ever were, are or were either fathers of their people, or heirs of such fathers, or usurpers of the right of such fathers,* Observations, 253. And here he makes *inheritance* or *usurpation* the only ways whereby kings come by this original *power:* but yet he tells us, *This fatherly empire, as it was of itself hereditary, so it was alienable by patent, and seizable by an usurper,* Observations, 190. So then here inheritance, grant, or usurpation, will convey it. And last of all, which is most admirable, he tells us, p. 100. *It skills not which way kings come by their power, whether by election, donation, succession, or by any other means; for it is still the manner of the government by supreme power, that makes them properly kings, and not the means of obtaining their crowns.* Which I think is a full answer to all his whole *hypothesis* and discourse about *Adam*'s royal authority, as the fountain from which all princes were to derive theirs: and he might have spared the trouble of speaking so much as he does, up and down, of heirs and inheritance, if to make any one *properly a king,* needs no more but *governing by supreme power, and it matters not by what means he came by it.*

§. 79. By this notable way, our author may make *Oliver* as *properly king,* as any one else he could think of: and had he had the happiness to live under *Massanello*'s government, he could not by this his own rule have forborn to have done homage to him, with *O king live for ever,* since the manner of his government by supreme power, made him *properly* king, who was but the day before *properly* a fisherman. And if *Don Quixote* had taught his squire to govern with supreme authority, our author no doubt could have made a most loyal subject in *Sancho Pancha*'s *island;* and he must needs have deserved some preferment in such governments, since I think he is the first politician, who, pretending to settle government upon its true basis, and to establish the thrones of lawful princes, ever told the world, That he was *properly a king, whose manner of government was by supreme power, by what means soever he obtained it;* which in plain *English* is to say, that regal and supreme power is properly and truly his, who can by any means seize upon it; and if this be to be *properly a king,* I wonder how he came to think of, or where he will find, an *usurper.*

§. 80. This is so strange a doctrine, that the surprise of it hath made me pass by, without their due reflection, the contradictions he runs into, by making sometimes *inheritance* alone, sometimes only *grant* or *inheritance,* sometimes only *inheritance* or *usurpation,* sometimes all these three, and at last *election,* or *any other means,* added to them, the ways whereby *Adam*'s royal *authority,* that is, his right to supreme rule, could be conveyed down to future kings and governors, so as to give them a title to the obedience and subjection of the people. But these contradictions lie so open, that the very reading of our author's own words will discover them to any ordinary understanding; and though what I have quoted out of him (with abundance more of the same strain and coherence, which might be found in him) might well excuse me from any farther trouble in this argument, yet having proposed to myself, to examine the main parts of his doctrine, I shall a little more particularly consider how *inheritance, grant, usurpation* or *election,* can any way make out government in the world upon his principles; or derive to any one a right of empire, from this regal authority of *Adam,* had it been never so well proved, that he had been absolute monarch, and lord of the whole world.

CHAPTER IX.

Of Monarchy, by Inheritance from Adam.

§. 81. Though it be never so plain, that there ought to be government in the world, nay, should all men be of our author's mind, that divine appointment had ordained it to be *monarchical;* yet, since men cannot obey any thing, that cannot command; and ideas of government in the fancy, though never so perfect, though never so right, cannot give laws, nor prescribe rules to the actions of men; it would be of no behoof for the settling of order, and establishment of government in its exercise and use amongst men, unless there were a way also taught how to know the person, to whom it belonged to have this power, and exercise this dominion over others. It is in vain then to talk of subjection and obedience without telling us whom we are to obey: for were I never so fully persuaded that there ought to be magistracy and rule in the world; yet I am never the less at liberty still, till it appears who is the person that hath right to my obedience; since, if there be no marks to know him by, and distinguish him that hath right to rule from other men, it may be myself, as well as any other. And therefore, though submission to government be every one's duty, yet since that signifies nothing but submitting to the direction and laws of such men as have authority to command, it is not enough to make a man a subject, to convince him that there is *regal power* in the world; but there must be ways of designing, and knowing the person to whom this *regal power* of right belongs: and a man can never be obliged in conscience to submit to any power, unless he can be satisfied who is the person who has a right to exercise that power over him. If this were not so, there would be no distinction between pirates and lawful princes; he that has force is without any more ado to be obeyed, and crowns and scepters would become the inheritance only of violence and rapine. Men too might as often and as innocently change their governors, as they do their physicians, if the person cannot be known who has a right to direct me, and whose prescriptions I am bound to follow. To settle therefore men's consciences, under an obligation to obedience, it is necessary that they know not only, that there is a power somewhere in the world, but the person who by right is vested with this power over them.

§. 82. How successful our author has been in his attempts, to set up a *monarchical absolute power* in *Adam,* the reader may judge by what has been already said; but were that *absolute monarchy* as clear as our author would desire it, as I presume it is the contrary, yet it could be of no use to the government of mankind now in the world, unless he also make out these two things.

First, That this *power of Adam* was not to end with him, but was upon his decease conveyed intire to some other person, and so on to posterity.

Secondly, That the princes and rulers now on earth are possessed of this *power of Adam,* by a right way of conveyance derived to them.

§. 83. If the first of these fail, the *power of Adam,* were it never so great, never so certain, will signify nothing to the present government and societies in the world; but we must seek out some other original of power for the government of politys than this of *Adam,* or else there will be none at all in the world. If the latter fail, it will destroy the authority of the present governors, and absolve the people from subjection to them, since they, having no better a claim than others to that power, which is alone the fountain of all authority, can have no title to rule over them.

§. 84. Our author, having fancied an absolute sovereignty in *Adam,* mentions several ways of its conveyance to princes, that were to be his successors; but that which he chiefly insists on, is that of *inheritance,* which occurs so often in his several discourses; and I having in the foregoing chapter quoted several of these passages, I shall not need here again to repeat them. This sovereignty he erects, as has been said, upon a double foundation, *viz.* that of *property,* and that of *fatherhood.* One was the right he was supposed to have in all creatures, a right to possess the earth with the beasts, and other inferior ranks of things in it, for his private use, exclusive of all other men. The other was the right he was supposed to have, to rule and govern men, all the rest of mankind.

§. 85. In both these rights, there being supposed an exclusion of all other men, it must be upon some reason peculiar to *Adam,* that they must both be founded.

That of his *property* our author supposes to arise from God's immediate *donation, Gen.* i. 28. and that of *fatherhood* from the act of *begetting:* now in all inheritance, if the heir succeed not to the reason upon which his father's right was founded, he cannot succeed to the right which followeth from it. For example, *Adam* had a right of property in the creatures upon the *donation* and *grant* of God almighty, who was lord and proprietor of them all: let this be so as our author tells us, yet upon his death his heir can have no title to them, no such right of property in them, unless the same reason, *viz.* God's *donation,* vested a right in the *heir* too: for if *Adam* could have had no property in, nor use of the creatures, without this positive *donation* from God, and this *donation* were only personally to *Adam,* his *heir* could have no right by it; but upon his death it must revert to God, the lord and owner again; for positive grants give no title farther than the express words convey it, and by which only it is held. And thus, if as our author himself contends, that *donation, Gen.* i. 28. were made only to *Adam* personally, his heir could not succeed to his property in the creatures; and if it were a donation to any but *Adam,* let it be shewn, that it was to his heir in our author's sense, *i. e.* to one of his children, exclusive of all the rest.

§. 86. But not to follow our author too far out of the way, the plain of the case is this. God having made man, and planted in him, as in all other animals, a strong desire of self-preservation; and furnished the world with things fit for food and raiment, and other necessaries of life, subservient to his design, that man should live and abide for some time upon the face of the earth, and not that so curious and wonderful a piece of workmanship, by his own negligence, or want of necessaries, should perish again, presently after a few moments continuance; God, I say, having made man and the world thus, spoke to him, (that is) directed him by his senses and reason, as he did the inferior animals by their sense and instinct, which were serviceable for his subsistence, and given him as the means of his *preservation.* And therefore I doubt not, but before these words were pronounced, i. *Gen.* 28, 29. (if they must be understood literally to have been spoken) and without any such verbal *donation,* man had a right to an use of the creatures, by the will and grant of God: for the desire, strong desire of preserving his life and being, having been planted in him as a principle of action by God himself, reason, *which was the voice of God in him,* could not but teach him and assure him, that pursuing that natural inclination he had to preserve his being, he followed the will of his maker, and therefore had a right to make use of those creatures, which by his reason or senses he could discover would be serviceable thereunto. And thus man's *property* in the creatures was founded upon the right he had to make use of those things that were necessary or useful to his being.

§. 87. This being the reason and foundation of *Adam's property,* gave the same title, on the same ground, to all his children, not only after his death, but in his life-time: so that here was no privilege of his *heir* above his other children, which could exclude them from an equal right to the use of the inferior creatures, for the comfortable preservation of their beings, which is all the *property* man hath in them; and so *Adam*'s sovereignty built on *property,* or, as our author calls it, *private dominion,* comes to nothing. Every man had a right to the creatures, by the same title *Adam* had, *viz.* by the right every one had to take care of, and provide for their subsistence: and thus men had a right in common, *Adam*'s children in common with him. But if any one had began, and made himself a property in any particular thing, (which how he, or any one else, could do, shall be shewn in another place) that thing, that possession, if he disposed not otherwise of it by his positive grant, descended naturally to his children, and they had a right to succeed to it, and possess it.

§. 88. It might reasonably be asked here, how come children by this right of possessing, before any other, the properties of their parents upon their decease? for it being personally the parents, when they die, without actually transferring their right to another, why does it not return again to the common stock of mankind? It will perhaps be answered, that common consent hath disposed of it to their children. Common practice, we see indeed, does so dispose of it; but we cannot say, that it is the common consent of mankind; for that hath never been asked, nor actually given; and if common tacit consent hath established it, it would make but a positive, and not a natural right of children to inherit the goods of their parents: but where the practice is universal, it is reasonable to think the cause is natural. The ground then I think to be this. The first and strongest desire God planted in men, and wrought into the very principles of their nature, being that of self-preservation, that is the foundation of a right to the creatures for the particular support and use of each individual person himself. But, next to this, God planted in men a strong desire also of propagating their kind, and continuing themselves in their posterity; and this gives children a title to share in the *property* of their parents, and a right to inherit their possessions. Men are not proprietors of what they have, meerly for themselves; their children have a title to part of it, and have their kind of right joined with their parents, in the possession which comes to be wholly their's, when death, having put an end to their parents use of it, hath taken them from their possessions; and this we call inheritance: men being by a like obligation bound to preserve what they have begotten, as to preserve themselves, their issue come to have a right in the goods they are possessed of. That children have such a right, is plain from the laws of God; and that men are convinced that children have such a right, is evident from the law of the land; both which laws require parents to provide for their children.

§. 89. For children being by the course of nature, born weak, and unable to provide for themselves, they have by the appointment of God himself, who hath thus ordered the course of nature, a right to be nourished and maintained by their parents; nay, a right not only to a bare subsistence, but to the conveniencies and comforts of life, as far as the conditions of their parents can afford it. Hence it comes, that when their parents leave the world, and so the care due to their children ceases, the effects of it are to extend as far as possibly they can, and the provisions they have made in their life-time, are understood to be intended, as nature requires they should, for their children, whom, after themselves, they are bound to provide for: though the dying parents, by express words, declare nothing about them, nature appoints the descent of their property to their children, who thus come to have a title, and natural right of inheritance to their fathers goods, which the rest of mankind cannot pretend to.

§. 90. Were it not for this right of being nourished and maintained by their parents, which God and nature has given to children, and obliged parents to as a duty, it would be reasonable, that the father should inherit the estate of his son, and be preferred in the inheritance before his grand-child: for to the grand-father there is due a long score of care and expences laid out upon the breeding and education of his son, which one would think in justice ought to be paid. But that having been done in obedience to the same law, whereby he received nourishment and education from his own parents; this score of education, received from a man's father, is paid by taking care, and providing for his own children; is paid, I say, as much as is required of payment by alteration of property, unless present necessity of the parents require a return of goods for their necessary support and subsistence: for we are not now speaking of that reverence, acknowledgment, respect and honour, that is always due from children to their parents; but of possessions and commodities of life valuable by money. But though it be incumbent on parents to bring up and provide for their children, yet this debt to their children does not quite cancel the score due to their parents; but only is made by nature preferable to it: for the debt a man owes his father takes place, and gives the father a right to inherit the son's goods, where, for want of issue, the right of children doth not exclude that title. And therefore a man having a right to be maintained by his children, where he needs it; and to enjoy also the comforts of life from them, when the necessary provision due to them and their children will afford it; if his son die without issue, the father has a right in nature to possess his goods, and inherit his estate, (whatever the municipal laws of some countries may absurdly direct otherwise;) and so again his children and their issue from him; or, for want of such, his father and his issue. But where no such are to be found, *i. e.* no kindred, there we see the possessions of a private man revert to the community, and so in politic societies come into the hands of the public magistrate; but in the state of nature become again perfectly common, no body having a right to inherit them: nor can any one have a property in them, otherwise than in other things common by nature; of which I shall speak in its due place.

§. 91. I have been the larger, in shewing upon what ground children have a right to succeed to the possession of their fathers properties, not only because by it, it will appear, that if *Adam* had a property (a titular, insignificant, useless property; for it could be no better, for he was bound to nourish and maintain his children and posterity out of it) in the whole earth and its product, yet all his children coming to have, by the law of nature, and right of inheritance, a joint title, and right of property in it after his death, it could convey no right of sovereignty to any one of his posterity over the rest: since every one having a right of inheritance to his portion, they might enjoy their inheritance, or any part of it in common, or share it, or some parts of it, by division, as it best liked them. But no one could pretend to the whole inheritance, or any sovereignty supposed to accompany it; since a right of inheritance gave every one of the rest, as well as any one, a title to share in the goods of his father. Not only upon this account, I say, have I been so particular in examining the reason of children's inheriting the property of their fathers, but also because it will give us farther light in the inheritance of *rule* and *power,* which in countries where their particular municipal laws give the whole possession of land entirely to the first-born, and descent of power has gone so to men by this custom, some have been apt to be deceived into an opinion, that there was a natural or divine right of primogeniture, to both *estate* and *power;* and that the inheritance of both *rule* over men, and *property* in things, sprang from the same original, and were to descend by the same rules.

§. 92. Property, whose original is from the right a man has to use any of the inferior creatures, for the subsistence and comfort of his life, is for the benefit and sole advantage of the proprietor, so that he may even destroy the thing, that he has property in by his use of it, where need requires: but government being for the preservation of every man's right and property, by preserving him from the violence or injury of others, is for the good of the governed: for the magistrate's sword being for a *terror to evil doers,* and by that terror to inforce men to observe the positive laws of the society, made conformable to the laws of nature, for the public good, *i. e.* the good of every particular member of that society, as far as by common rules it can be provided for; the sword is not given the magistrate for his own good alone.

§. 93. Children therefore, as has been shewed, by the dependance they have on their parents for subsistence, have a right of inheritance to their fathers property, as that which belongs to them for their proper good and behoof, and therefore are fitly termed goods, wherein the first-born has not a sole or peculiar right by any law of God and nature, the younger children having an equal title with him, founded on that right they all have to maintenance, support, and comfort from their parents, and on nothing else. But government being for the benefit of the governed, and not the sole advantage of the governors, (but only for their's with the rest, as they make a part of that politic body, each of whose parts and members are taken care of, and directed in its peculiar functions for the good of the whole, by the laws of society) cannot be inherited by the same title, that children have to the goods of their father. The right a son has to be maintained and provided with the necessaries and conveniences of life out of his father's stock, gives him a right to succeed to his father's *property* for his own good; but this can give him no right to succeed also to the *rule,* which his father had over other men. All that a child has right to claim from his father is nourishment and education, and the things nature furnishes for the support of life: but he has no right to demand *rule* or *dominion* from him: he can subsist and receive from him the portion of good things, and advantages of education naturally due to him, without *empire* and *dominion.* That (if his father hath any) was vested in him, for the good and behoof of others: and therefore the son cannot claim or inherit it by a title, which is founded wholly on his own private good and advantage.

§. 94. We must know how the first ruler, from whom any one claims, came by his authority, upon what ground any one has *empire,* what his title is to it, before we can know who has a right to succeed him in it, and inherit it from him: if the agreement and consent of men first gave a scepter into any one's hand, or put a crown on his head, that also must direct its descent and conveyance; for the same authority, that made the first a lawful *ruler,* must make the second too, and so give right of succession: in this case inheritance, or primogeniture, can in its self have no right, no pretence to it, any farther than that consent, which established the form of the government, hath so settled the succession. And thus we see, the succession of crowns, in several countries, places it on different heads, and he comes by right of succession to be a prince in one place, who would be a subject in another.

§. 95. If God, by his positive grant and revealed declaration, first gave *rule* and *dominion* to any man, he that will claim by that title, must have the same positive grant of God for his succession: for if that has not directed the course of its descent and conveyance down to others, no body can succeed to this title of the first ruler. Children have no right of inheritance to this; and primogeniture can lay no claim to it, unless God, the author of this constitution, hath so ordained it. Thus we see, the pretensions of *Saul*'s family, who received his crown from the immediate appointment of God, ended with his reign; and *David,* by the same title that *Saul* reigned, *viz.* God's appointment, succeeded in his throne, to the exclusion of *Jonathan,* and all pretensions of paternal inheritance: and if *Solomon* had a right to succeed his father, it must be by some other title, than that of primogeniture. A *cadet,* or sister's son, must have the preference in succession, if he has the same title the first lawful prince had: and in dominion that has its foundation only in the positive appointment of God himself, *Benjamin,* the youngest, must have the inheritance of the crown, if God so direct, as well as one of that tribe had the first possession.

§. 96. If *paternal right,* the act of *begetting,* give a man *rule* and *dominion,* inheritance or primogeniture can give no title: for he that cannot succeed to his father's title, which was *begetting,* cannot succeed to that power over his brethren, which his father had by paternal right over them. But of this I shall have occasion to say more in another place. This is plain in the mean time, that any government, whether supposed to be at first founded in *paternal right, consent of the people,* or the *positive appointment of God himself,* which can supersede either of the other, and so begin a new government upon a new foundation; I say, any government began upon either of these, can by right of succession come to those only, who have the title of him they succeed to: power founded on *contract* can descend only to him, who has right by that contract: power founded on *begetting,* he only can have that *begets;* and power founded on the positive *grant* or donation of God, he only can have by right of succession, to whom that grant directs it.

§. 97. From what I have said, I think this is clear, that a right to the use of the creatures, being founded originally in the right a man has to subsist and enjoy the conveniencies of life; and the natural right children have to inherit the goods of their parents, being founded in the right they have to the same subsistence and commodities of life, out of the stock of their parents, who are therefore taught by natural love and tenderness to provide for them, as a part of themselves; and all this being only for the good of the proprietor, or heir; it can be no reason for children's inheriting of *rule* and *dominion,* which has another original and a different end. Nor can primogeniture have any pretence to a right of solely inheriting either *property* or *power,* as we shall, in its due place, see more fully. It is enough to have shewed here, that *Adam*'s *property,* or *private dominion,* could not convey any sovereignty or rule to his heir, who not having a right to inherit all his father's possessions, could not thereby come to have any sovereignty over his brethren: and therefore, if any sovereignty on account of his *property* had been vested in *Adam,* which in truth there was not, yet it would have died with him.

§. 98. As *Adam*'s sovereignty, if, by virtue of being proprietor of the world, he had any authority over men, could not have been inherited by any of his children over the rest, because they had the same title to divide the inheritance, and every one had a right to a portion of his father's possessions; so neither could *Adam*'s sovereignty by right of *fatherhood,* if any such he had, descend to any one of his children: for it being, in our author's account, a right acquired by *begetting* to rule over those he had begotten, it was not a power possible to be inherited, because the right being consequent to, and built on, an act perfectly personal, made that power so too, and impossible to be inherited: for paternal power, being a natural right rising only from the relation of father and son, is as impossible to be inherited as the relation itself; and a man may pretend as well to inherit the conjugal power the husband, whose heir he is, had over his wife, as he can to inherit the paternal power of a father over his children: for the power of the husband being founded on contract, and the power of the father on *begetting,* he may as well inherit the power obtained by the conjugal contract, which was only personal, as he may the power obtained by begetting, which could reach no farther than the person of the begetter, unless begetting can be a title to power in him that does not beget.

§. 99. Which makes it a reasonable question to ask, whether *Adam,* dying before *Eve,* his heir, (suppose *Cain* or *Seth)* should have by right of inheriting *Adam*'s *fatherhood,* sovereign power over *Eve* his mother: for *Adam*'s *fatherhood* being nothing but a right he had to govern his children, because he begot them, he that inherits *Adam*'s *fatherhood,* inherits nothing, even in our author's sense, but the right *Adam* had to govern his children, because he begot them: so that the monarchy of the heir would not have taken in *Eve;* or if it did, it being nothing but the *fatherhood of Adam* descended by inheritance, the heir must have right to govern *Eve,* because *Adam* begot her; for *fatherhood* is nothing else.

§. 100. Perhaps it will be said with our author, that a man can alien his power over his child; and what may be transferred by compact, may be possessed by inheritance. I answer, a father cannot alien the power he has over his child: he may perhaps to some degrees forfeit it, but cannot transfer it; and if any other man acquire it, it is not by the father's grant, but by some act of his own. For example, a father, unnaturally careless of his child, sells or gives him to another man; and he again exposes him; a third man finding him, breeds up, cherishes, and provides for him as his own: I think in this case, no body will doubt, but that the greatest part of filial duty and subjection was here owing, and to be paid to this foster-father; and if any thing could be demanded from the child, by either of the other, it could be only due to his natural father, who perhaps might have forfeited his right to much of that duty comprehended in the command, *Honour your parents,* but could transfer none of it to another. He that purchased, and neglected the child, got by his purchase and grant of the father, no title to duty or honour from the child; but only he acquired it, who by his own authority, performing the office and care of a father, to the forlorn and perishing infant, made himself, by paternal care, a title to proportionable degrees of paternal power. This will be more easily admitted upon consideration of the nature of paternal power, for which I refer my reader to the second book.

§. 101. To return to the argument in hand; this is evident, That paternal power arising only from *begetting,* for in that our author places it alone, can neither be *transferred* nor *inherited:* and he that does not beget, can no more have paternal power, which arises from thence, than he can have a right to any thing, who performs not the condition, to which only it is annexed. If one should ask, by what law has a father power over his children? it will be answered, no doubt, by the law of nature, which gives such a power over them, to him that begets them. If one should ask likewise, by what law does our author's heir come by a right to inherit? I think it would be answered, by the law of nature too: for I find not that our author brings one word of scripture to prove the right of such an heir he speaks of. Why then the law of nature gives fathers paternal power over their children, because they did *beget* them; and the same law of nature gives the same paternal power to the heir over his brethren, who did not beget them: whence it follows, that either the father has not his paternal power by begetting, or else that the heir has it not at all; for it is hard to understand how the law of nature, which is the law of reason, can give the paternal power to the father over his children, for the only reason of *begetting;* and to the first-born over his brethren without this only reason, *i. e.*

for no reason at all: and if the eldest, by the law of nature, can inherit this paternal power, without the only reason that gives a title to it, so may the youngest as well as he, and a stranger as well as either; for where there is no reason for any one, as there is not, but for him that begets, all have an equal title. I am sure our author offers no reason; and when any body does, we shall see whether it will hold or no.

§. 102. In the mean time it is as good sense to say, that by the law of nature a man has right to inherit the property of another, because he is of kin to him, and is known to be of his blood; and therefore, by the same law of nature, an utter stranger to his blood has right to inherit his estate; as to say that, by the law of nature, he that begets them has paternal power over his children, and therefore, by the law of nature, the heir that begets them not, has this paternal power over them; or supposing the law of the land gave absolute power over their children, to such only who nursed them, and fed their children themselves, could any body pretend, that this law gave any one, who did no such thing, absolute power over those, who were not his children?

§. 103. When therefore it can be shewed, that conjugal power can belong to him that is not an husband, it will also I believe be proved, that our author's paternal power, acquired by begetting, may be inherited by a son; and that a brother, as heir to his father's power, may have paternal power over his brethren, and by the same rule conjugal power too: but till then, I think we may rest satisfied, that the paternal power of *Adam,* this sovereign authority of *fatherhood,* were there any such, could not descend to, nor be inherited by, his next heir. *Fatherly power,* I easily grant our author, if it will do him any good, can never be lost, because it will be as long in the world as there are fathers: but none of them will have *Adam*'s paternal power, or derive their's from him; but every one will have his own, by the same title *Adam* had his, *viz.* by *begetting,* but not by inheritance, or succession, no more than husbands have their conjugal power by inheritance from *Adam*. And thus we see, as *Adam* had no such *property,* no such *paternal power,* as gave him *sovereign* jurisdiction over mankind; so likewise his sovereignty built upon either of these titles, if he had any such, could not have descended to his heir, but must have ended with him. *Adam* therefore, as has been proved, being neither monarch, nor his imaginary monarchy hereditable, the power which is now in the world, is not that which was *Adam*'s, since all that *Adam* could have upon our author's grounds, either of *property* or *fatherhood,* necessarily died with him, and could not be conveyed to posterity by inheritance. In the next place we will consider, whether *Adam* had any such heir, to inherit his power, as our author talks of.

CHAPTER X.

Of the Heir to Adam's Monarchical Power.

§. 104. OUR author tells us, Observations, 253. *That it is a truth undeniable, that there cannot be any multitude of men whatsoever, either great or small, tho' gathered together from the several corners and remotest regions of the world, but that in the same multitude, considered by its self, there is one man amongst them, that in nature hath a right to be king of all the rest, as being the next heir to* Adam, *and all the other subjects to him: every man by nature is a king or a subject.* And again, p. 20. *If* Adam *himself were still living, and now ready to die, it is certain that there is one man, and but one in the world, who is next heir.* Let this *multitude of men* be, if our author pleases, all the princes upon the earth, there will then be, by our author's rule, *one amongst them, that in nature hath a right to be king of all the rest, as being the right heir to* Adam; an excellent way to establish the thrones of princes, and settle the obedience of their subjects, by setting up an hundred, or perhaps a thousand titles (if there be so many princes in the world) against any king now reigning, each as good, upon our author's grounds, as his who wears the crown. If this right of *heir* carry any weight with it, if it be the *ordinance of God,* as our author seems to tells us, *Observations,* 244. must not all be subject to it, from the highest to the lowest? Can those who wear the name of princes, without having the right of being *heirs to* Adam, demand obedience from their subjects by this title, and not be bound to pay it by the same law? Either governments in the world are not to be claimed, and held by this title of *Adam*'s heir; and then the starting of it is to no purpose, the being or not being *Adam*'s heir signifies nothing as to the title of dominion: or if it really be, as our author says, the true title to government and sovereignty, the first thing to be done, is to find out this true heir of *Adam,* seat him in his throne, and then all the kings and princes of the world ought to come and resign up their *crowns* and *scepters* to him, as things that belong no more to them, than to any of their subjects.

§. 105.For either this right in nature, of *Adam*'s heir, to be king over all the race of men, (for all together they make one *multitude*) is a right not necessary to the making of a lawful king, and so there may be lawful kings without it, and then kings titles and power depend not on it; or else all the kings in the world but one are not lawful kings, and so have no right to obedience: either this title of heir to *Adam* is that whereby kings hold their crowns, and have a right to subjection from their subjects, and then one only can have it, and the rest being subjects can require no obedience from other men, who are but their fellow subjects; or else it is not the title whereby kings rule, and have a right to obedience from their subjects, and then kings are kings without it, and this dream of the natural sovereignty of *Adam*'s heir is of no use to obedience and government: for if kings have a right to dominion, and the obedience of their subjects, who are not, nor can possibly be, heirs to *Adam,* what use is there of such a title, when we are obliged to obey without it? If kings, who are not heirs to *Adam,* have no right to sovereignty, we are all free, till our author, or any body for him, will shew us *Adam*'s right heir. If there be but one heir of *Adam,* there can be but one lawful king in the world, and no body in conscience can be obliged to obedience till it be resolved who that is; for it may be any one, who is not known to be of a younger house, and all others have equal titles. If there be more than one heir of *Adam,* every one is his heir, and so every one has regal power: for if two sons can be heirs together, then all the sons are equally heirs, and so all are heirs, being all sons, or sons sons of *Adam.* Betwixt these two the right of heir cannot stand; for by it either but one only man, or all men are kings. Take which you please, it dissolves the bonds of government and obedience; since, if all men are heirs, they can owe obedience to no body; if only one, no body can be obliged to pay obedience to him, till he be known, and his title made out.

CHAPTER XI.

Who HEIR?

§. 106. THE great question which in all ages has disturbed mankind, and brought on them the greatest part of those mischiefs which have ruined cities, depopulated countries, and disordered the peace of the world, has been, not whether there be power in the world, nor whence it came, but who should have it. The settling of this point being of no smaller moment than the security of princes, and the peace and welfare of their estates and kingdoms, a reformer of politics, one would think, should lay this sure, and be very clear in it: for if this remain disputable, all the rest will be to very little purpose; and the skill used in dressing up power with all the splendor and temptation absoluteness can add to it, without shewing who has a right to have it, will serve only to give a greater edge to man's natural ambition, which of its self is but too keen. What can this do but set men on the more eagerly to scramble, and so lay a sure and lasting foundation of endless contention and disorder, instead of that peace and tranquillity, which is the business of government, and the end of human society?

§. 107. This designation of the person our author is more than ordinary obliged to take care of, because he, affirming that *the assignment of civil power is by divine institution,* hath made the conveyance as well as the power itself sacred: so that no consideration, no act or art of man, can divert it from that person, to whom, by this divine right, it is assigned; no necessity or contrivance can substitute another person in his room: for if the *assignment of civil power be by divine institution,* and *Adam*'s *heir* be he to whom it is thus assigned, as in the foregoing chapter our author tells us, it would be as much sacrilege for any one to be king, who was not *Adam*'s heir, as it would have been amongst the *Jews,* for any one to have been *priest,* who had not been of *Aaron*'s posterity: for *not only* the priesthood *in general being by divine institution, but the assignment of it* to the sole line and posterity of *Aaron,* made it impossible to be enjoyed or exercised by any one, but those persons who were the off-spring of *Aaron:* whose succession therefore was carefully observed, and by that the persons who had a right to the priesthood certainly known.

§. 108. Let us see then what care our author has taken, to make us know who is this *heir,* who *by divine institution has a right to be king over all men.* The first account of him we meet with is, p. 12. in these words: *This subjection of children, being the fountain of all regal authority, by the ordination of God himself; it follows, that civil power, not only in general, is by divine institution, but even the assignment of it, specifically to the eldest parents.* Matters of such consequence as this is, should be in plain words, as little liable, as might be, to doubt or equivocation; and I think, if language be capable of expressing any thing distinctly and clearly, that of kindred, and the several degrees of nearness of blood, is one. It were therefore to be wished, that our author had used a little more intelligible expressions here, that we might have better known, who it is, to whom the *assignment of civil power* is made by *divine institution;* or at least would have told us what he meant by *eldest parents:* for I believe, if land had been assigned or granted to him, and the *eldest parents* of his family, he would have thought it had needed an interpreter; and it would scarce have been known to whom next it belonged.

§. 109. In propriety of speech, (and certainly propriety of speech is necessary in a discourse of this nature) *eldest parents* signifies either the eldest men and women that have had children, or those who have longest had issue; and then our author's assertion will be, that those fathers and mothers, who have been longest in the world, or longest fruitful, have by *divine institution* a right to *civil power.* If there be any absurdity in this, our author must answer for it: and if his meaning be different from my explication, he is to be blamed, that he would not speak it plainly. This I am sure, *parents* cannot signify heirs male, nor *eldest parents* an infant child: who yet may sometimes be the true heir, if there can be but one. And we are hereby still as much at a loss, who *civil power* belongs to, notwithstanding this *assignment by divine institution,* as if there had been no such *assignment* at all, or our author had said nothing of it. This of *eldest parents* leaving us more in the dark, who by *divine institution* has a right to *civil power,* than those who never heard any thing at all of *heir,* or descent, of which our author is so full. And though the chief matter of his writing be to teach obedience to those, who have a right to it, which he tells us is conveyed by descent, yet who those are, to whom this right by descent belongs, he leaves, like the philosophers stone in politics, out of the reach of any one to discover from his writings.

§. 110. This obscurity cannot be imputed to want of language in so great a master of style as Sir *Robert* is, when he is resolved with himself what he would say: and therefore, I fear, finding how hard it would be to settle rules of descent by divine institution, and how little it would be to his purpose, or conduce to the clearing and establishing the titles of princes, if such rules of descent were settled, he chose rather to content himself with doubtful and general terms, which might make no ill found in mens ears, who were willing to be pleased with them, rather than offer any clear rules of descent of this *fatherhood* of *Adam,* by which men's consciences might be satisfied to whom it descended, and know the persons who had a right to regal power, and with it to their obedience.

§. 111. How else is it possible, that laying so much stress, as he does, upon *descent,* and *Adam*'s *heir, next heir, true heir,* he should never tell us what *heir* means, nor the way to know who the *next* or *true heir* is? This, I do not remember, he does any where expresly handle; but, where it comes in his way, very warily and doubtfully touches; though it be so necessary, that without it all discourses of government and obedience upon his principles would be to no purpose, and *fatherly power,* never so well made out, will be of no use to any body. Hence he tells us, *Observations,* 244. *That not only the constitution of power in general, but the limitation of it to one kind,* (i. e.) *monarchy, and the determination of it to the individual person and line of* Adam, *are all three ordinances of God; neither* Eve *nor her children could either limit* Adam's *power, or join others with him; and what was given unto* Adam *was given in his person to his posterity.* Here again our author informs us, that the *divine ordinance* hath limited the descent of *Adam*'s monarchical power. To whom? *To* Adam'*s line and posterity,* says our author. A notable *limitation,* a *limitation* to all mankind: for if our author can find any one amongst mankind, that is not of the *line* and *posterity* of *Adam,* he may perhaps tell him, who this next heir of *Adam* is: but for us, I despair how this *limitation* of *Adam*'s empire to his *line* and *posterity* will help us to find out *one heir.* This *limitation* indeed of our author will save those the labour, who would look for him amongst the race of brutes, if any such there were; but will very little contribute to the discovery of *one next heir* amongst men, though it make a short and easy determination of the question about the descent of *Adam*'s regal power, by telling us, that the *line* and *posterity* of *Adam* is to have it, that is, in plain *English,* any one may have it, since there is no person living that hath not the title of being of the *line* and *posterity* of *Adam;* and while it keeps there, it keeps within our author's limitation by God's ordinance. Indeed, p. 19. he tells us, that *such heirs are not only lords of their own children, but of their brethren;* whereby, and by the words following, which we shall consider anon, he seems to insinuate, that the eldest son is *heir;* but he no where, that I know, says it in direct words, but by the instances of *Cain* and *Jacob,* that there follow, we may allow this to be so far his opinion concerning heirs, that where there are divers children, the eldest son has the right to be *heir.* That primogeniture cannot give any title to paternal power, we have already shewed. That a father may have a natural right to some kind of power over his children, is easily granted; but that an elder brother has so over his brethren, remains to be proved: God or nature has not any where, that I know, placed such jurisdiction in the first-born; nor can reason find any such natural superiority amongst brethren. The law of *Moses* gave a double portion of the goods and possessions to the eldest; but we find not any where that naturally, or by *God*'s *institution,* superiority or dominion belonged to him, and the instances there brought by our author are but slender proofs of a right to civil power and dominion in the first-born, and do rather shew the contrary.

§. 112. His words are in the forecited place: *And therefore we find God told* Cain *of his brother* Abel; *his desire shall be subject unto thee, and thou shalt rule over him.* To which I answer,

1. These words of God to *Cain,* are by many interpreters, with great reason, understood in a quite different sense than what our author uses them in.

2. Whatever was meant by them, it could not be, that *Cain,* as elder, had a natural dominion over *Abel;* for the words are conditional, *If thou dost well;* and so personal to *Cain:* and whatever was signified by them, did depend on his carriage, and not follow his birth-right; and therefore could by no means be an establishment of dominion in the first-born in general: for before this *Abel* had his *distinct territories by right of private dominion,* as our author himself confesses, *Observations,* 210. which he could not have had to the prejudice of the heirs title, *if by divine institution, Cain* as heir were to inherit all his father's dominion.

3. If this were intended by God as the charter of primogeniture, and the grant of dominion to elder brothers in general as such, by right of inheritance, we might expect it should have included all his brethren: for we may well suppose, *Adam,* from whom the world was to be peopled, had by this time, that these were grown up to be men, more sons than these two: whereas *Abel* himself is not so much as named; and the words in the original can scarce, with any good construction, be applied to him.

4. It is too much to build a doctrine of so mighty consequence upon so doubtful and obscure a place of scripture, which may be well, nay better, understood in a quite different sense, and so can be but an ill proof, being as doubtful as the thing to be proved by it; especially when there is nothing else in scripture or reason to be found, that favours or supports it.

§. 113. It follows, p. 19. *Accordingly when* Jacob *bought his brother's birth-right,* Isaac *blessed him thus; Be lord over thy brethren, and let the sons of thy mother bow before thee.* Another instance, I take it, brought by our author to evince dominion due to birth-right, and an admirable one it is: for it must be no ordinary way of reasoning in a man, that is pleading for the natural power of kings, and against all compact, to bring for proof of it, an example, where his own account of it founds all the right upon compact, and settles empire in the younger brother, unless buying and selling be no compact; for he tells us, *when* Jacob *bought his brother's birthright.* But passing by that, let us consider the history itself, with what use our author makes of it, and we shall find these following mistakes about it.

1. That our author reports this, as if *Isaac* had given *Jacob* this blessing, immediately upon his purchasing the *birth-right;* for he says, *when Jacob bought, Isaac blessed him;* which is plainly otherwise in the scripture: for it appears, there was a distance of time between, and if we will take the story in the order it lies, it must be no small distance; all *Isaac*'s sojourning in *Gerar,* and transactions with *Abimelech, Gen.* xxvi. coming between; *Rebecca* being then beautiful, and consequently young; but *Isaac,* when he blessed *Jacob,* was old and decrepit: and *Esau* also complains of *Jacob, Gen.* xxvii. 36. that *two times* he had supplanted him; *He took away my birth-right,* says he, *and behold now he hath taken away my blessing;* words, that I think signify distance of time and difference of action.

2. Another mistake of our author's is, that he supposes *Isaac* gave *Jacob the blessing,* and bid him be *lord over his brethren,* because he had the *birth-right;* for our author brings this example to prove, that he that has the *birth-right,* has thereby a right to *be lord over his brethren.* But it is also manifest by the text, that *Isaac* had no consideration of *Jacob*'s having bought the birth-right; for when he blessed him, he considered him not as *Jacob,* but took him for *Esau.* Nor did *Esau* understand any such connection between *birth-right* and the *blessing;* for he says, *He hath supplanted me these two times, he took away my birth-right, and behold now he hath taken away my blessing:* whereas had the *blessing,* which was to be *lord over his brethren,* belonged to the *birth-right, Esau* could not have complained of this second, as a cheat, *Jacob* having got nothing but what *Esau* had sold him, when he sold him his *birth-right;* so that it is plain, dominion, if these words signify it, was not understood to belong to the *birth-right.*

§. 114. And that in those days of the patriarchs, dominion was not understood to be the right of the heir, but only a greater portion of goods, is plain from *Gen.* xxi. 10. for *Sarah,* taking *Isaac* to be heir, says, *Cast out this bondwoman and her son, for the son of this bondwoman shall not be heir with my son:* whereby could be meant nothing, but that he should not have a pretence to an equal share of his father's estate after his death, but should have his portion presently, and be gone. Accordingly we read, *Gen.* xxv. 5, 6. That *Abraham gave all that he had unto Isaac, but unto the sons of the concubines which Abraham had, Abraham gave gifts, and sent them away from Isaac his son, while he yet lived.* That is, *Abraham* having given portions to all his other sons, and sent them away, that which he had reserved, being the greatest part of his substance, *Isaac* as heir possessed after his death: but by being heir, he had no right to be *lord over his brethren;* for if he had, why should *Sarah* endeavour to rob him of one of his *subjects,* or lessen the number of his *slaves,* by desiring to have *Ishmael* sent away?

§. 115. Thus, as under the law, the privilege of *birth-right* was nothing but a double portion: so we see that before *Moses,* in the patriarchs time, from whence our author pretends to take his model, there was no knowledge, no thought, that birth-right gave rule or empire, paternal or kingly authority, to any one over his brethren. If this be not plain enough in the story of *Isaac* and *Ishmael,* he that will look into 1 *Chron.* v. 12. may there read these words: *Reuben was the first-born; but forasmuch as he defiled his father's bed, his birth-right was given unto the sons of Joseph, the son of Israel: and the genealogy is not to be reckoned after the birth-right; for Judah prevailed above his brethren, and of him came the chief ruler; but the birth-right was Joseph*'s. What this birth-right was, *Jacob* blessing *Joseph, Gen.* xlviii. 22. telleth us in these words, *Moreover I have given thee one portion above thy brethren, which I took out of the hand of the Amorite, with my sword and with my bow.* Whereby it is not only plain, that the birth-right was nothing but a double portion; but the text in *Chronicles* is express against our author's doctrine, and shews that dominion was no part of the birth-right; for it tells us, that *Joseph* had the birth-right, but *Judah* the dominion. One would think our author were very fond of the very name of *birth-right,* when he brings this instance of *Jacob* and *Esau,* to prove that dominion belongs to the heir over his brethren.

§. 116. 1. Because it will be but an ill example to prove, that dominion by God's ordination belonged to the eldest son, because *Jacob* the youngest here had it, let him come by it how he would: for if it prove any thing, it can only prove, against our author, that the *assignment of dominion to the eldest is not by divine institution,* which would then be unalterable: for if by the law of God, or nature, absolute power and empire belongs to the eldest son and his heirs, so that they are supreme monarchs, and all the rest of their brethren slaves, our author gives us reason to doubt whether the eldest son has a power to part with it, to the prejudice of his posterity, since he tells us, *Observations,* 158. That *in grants and gifts that have their original from God or nature, no inferior power of man can limit, or make any law of prescription against them.*

§. 117. 2. Because this place, *Gen.* xxvii. 29. brought by our author, concerns not at all the dominion of one brother over the other, nor the subjection of *Esau* to *Jacob:* for it is plain in the history, that *Esau* was never subject to *Jacob,* but lived apart in mount *Seir,* where he founded a distinct people and government, and was himself prince over them, as much as *Jacob* was in his own family. This text, if considered, can never be understood of *Esau* himself, or the personal dominion of *Jacob* over him: for the words *brethren* and *sons of thy mother,* could not be used literally by *Isaac,* who knew *Jacob* had only one brother; and these words are so far from being true in a literal sense, or establishing any dominion in *Jacob* over *Esau,* that in the story we find the quite contrary, for *Gen.* xxxii. *Jacob* several times calls *Esau* lord, and himself his servant; and *Gen.* xxxiii. *he bowed himself seven times to the ground to* Esau. Whether *Esau* then were a subject and vassal (nay, as our author tells us, all subjects are slaves) to *Jacob,* and *Jacob* his sovereign prince by birth-right, I leave the reader to judge; and to believe if he can, that these words of *Isaac, Be lord over thy brethren, and let thy mother's sons bow down to thee,* confirmed *Jacob* in a sovereignty over *Esau,* upon the account of the *birth-right* he had got from him.

§. 118. He that reads the story of *Jacob* and *Esau,* will find there was never any jurisdiction or authority, that either of them had over the other after their father's death: they lived with the friendship and equality of brethren, neither *lord,* neither *slave* to his brother; but independent each of other, were both heads of their distinct families, where they received no laws from one another, but lived separately, and were the roots out of which sprang two distinct people under two distinct governments. This blessing then of *Isaac,* whereon our author would build the dominion of the elder brother, signifies no more, but what *Rebecca* had been told from God, *Gen.* xxv. 23. *Two nations are in thy womb, and two manner of people shall be separated from thy bowels, and the one people shall be stronger than the other people, and the elder shall serve the younger;* and so *Jacob* blessed *Judah, Gen.* xlix. and gave him the *scepter* and *dominion,* from whence our author might have argued as well, that jurisdiction and dominion belongs to the third son over his brethren, as well as from this blessing of *Isaac,* that it belonged to *Jacob:* both these places contain only predictions of what should long after happen to their posterities, and not any declaration of the right of inheritance to dominion in either. And thus we have our author's two great and only arguments to prove, that *heirs are lords over their brethren.*

1. Because God tells *Cain, Gen.* iv. that however sin might set upon him, he ought or might be master of it: for the most learned interpreters understood the words of sin, and not of *Abel,* and give so strong reasons for it, that nothing can convincingly be inferred, from so doubtful a text, to our author's purpose.

2. Because in this of *Gen.* xxvii. *Isaac* foretels that the *Israelites,* the posterity of *Jacob,* should have dominion over the *Edomites,* the posterity of *Esau;* therefore says our author, *heirs are lords of their brethren:* I leave any one to judge of the conclusion.

§. 119. And now we see how our author has provided for the descending, and conveyance down of *Adam*'s monarchical power, or paternal dominion to posterity, by the inheritance of his *heir,* succeeding to all his father's authority, and becoming upon his death as much lord as his father was, *not only over his own children, but over his brethren,* and all descended from his father, and so *in infinitum.* But yet who this heir is, he does not once tell us; and all the light we have from him in this so fundamental a point, is only, that in his instance of *Jacob,* by using the word *birth-right,* as that which passed from *Esau* to *Jacob,* he leaves us to guess, that by heir, he means the eldest son; though I do not remember he any where mentions expresly the title of the first-born, but all along keeps himself under the shelter of the indefinite term *heir.* But taking it to be his meaning, that the eldest son is heir, (for if the eldest be not, there will be no pretence why the sons should not be all *heirs* alike) and so by right of primogeniture has dominion over his brethren; this is but one step towards the settlement of succession, and the difficulties remain still as much as ever, till he can shew us who is meant by right heir, in all those cases which may happen where the present possessor hath no son. This he silently passes over, and perhaps wisely too: for what can be wiser, after one has affirmed, that *the person having that power, as well as the power and form of government, is the ordinance of God, and by divine institution,* vid. *Observations,* 254. p. 12. than to be careful, not to start any question concerning the person, the resolution whereof will certainly lead him into a confession, that God and nature hath determined nothing about him? And if our author cannot shew who by right of nature, or a clear positive law of God, has the next right to inherit the dominion of this natural monarch he has been at such pains about, when he died without a son, he might have spared his pains in all the rest, it being more necessary for the settling men's consciences, and determining their subjection and allegiance, to shew them who by original right, superior and antecedent to the will, or any act of men, hath a title to this *paternal jurisdiction,* than it is to shew that by nature there was such a *jurisdiction;* it being to no purpose for me to know there is such a *paternal power,* which I ought, and am disposed to obey, unless, where there are many pretenders, I also know the person that is rightfully invested and endowed with it.

§. 120. For the main matter in question being concerning the duty of my obedience, and the obligation of conscience I am under to pay it to him that is of right my lord and ruler, I must know the person that this right of paternal power resides in, and so impowers him to claim obedience from me: for let it be true what he says, p. 12. That *civil power not only in general is by divine institution, but even the assignment of it specially to the eldest parents;* and *Observations,* 254. *That not only the power or right of government, but the form of the power of governing, and the person having that power, are all the ordinance of God;* yet unless he shew us in all cases who is this person, *ordained* by God, who is this *eldest parent;* all his abstract notions of monarchical power will signify just nothing, when they are to be reduced to practice, and men are conscientiously to pay their obedience: for *paternal jurisdiction* being not the thing to be obeyed, because it cannot command, but is only that which gives one man a right which another hath not, and if it come by inheritance, another man cannot have, to command and be obeyed; it is ridiculous to say, I pay obedience to the *paternal power,* when I obey him, to whom paternal power gives no right to my obedience: for he can have no divine right to my obedience, who cannot shew his divine right to the power of ruling over me, as well as that by divine right there is such a power in the world.

§. 121. And hence not being able to make out any prince's title to government, as heir to *Adam,* which therefore is of no use, and had been better let alone, he is fain to resolve all into present possession, and makes civil obedience as due to an *usurper,* as to a lawful king; and thereby the *usurper*'s title as good. His words are, *Observations,* 253. and they deserve to be remembered: *If an usurper dispossess the true heir, the subjects obedience to the fatherly power must go along, and wait upon God's providence.* But I shall leave his title of usurpers to be examined in its due place, and desire my sober reader to consider what thanks princes owe such politics as this, which can suppose *paternal power* (*i. e.*) a right to government in the hands of a *Cade,* or a *Cromwell;* and so all obedience being due to paternal power, the obedience of subjects will be due to them, by the same right, and upon as good grounds, as it is to lawful princes; and yet this, as dangerous a doctrine as it is, must necessarily follow from making all political power to be nothing else, but *Adam*'s paternal power by right and divine *institution,* descending from him without being able to shew to whom it descended, or who is heir to it.

§. 122. To settle government in the world, and to lay obligations to obedience on any man's conscience, it is as necessary (supposing with our author that all power be nothing but the being possessed of *Adam's fatherhood)* to satisfy him, who has a right to this *power,* this *fatherhood,* when the possessor dies without sons to succeed immediately to it, as it was to tell him, that upon the death of the father, the eldest son had a right to it: for it is still to be remembered, that the great question is, (and that which our author would be thought to contend for, if he did not sometimes forget it) what persons have a right to be obeyed, and not whether there be a power in the world, which is to be called *paternal,* without knowing in whom it resides: for so it be a power, *i. e.* right to govern, it matters not, whether it be termed *paternal* or *regal, natural* or *acquired;* whether you call it *supreme fatherhood,* or *supreme brotherhood,* will be all one, provided we know who has it.

§. 123. I go on then to ask, whether in the inheriting of this *paternal power,* this *supreme fatherhood,* the grandson by a daughter hath a right before a nephew by a brother? Whether the grandson by the eldest son, being an infant, before the younger son, a man and able? Whether the daughter before the uncle? or any other man, descended by a male line? Whether a grandson by a younger daughter, before a grand-daughter by an elder daughter? Whether the elder son by a concubine, before a younger son by a wife? From whence also will arise many questions of legitimation, and what in nature is the difference betwixt a wife and a concubine? for as to the municipal or positive laws of men, they can signify nothing here. It may farther be asked, Whether the eldest son, being a fool, shall inherit this *paternal power,* before the younger, a wise man? and what degree of folly it must be that shall exclude him? and who shall be judge of it? Whether the son of a fool, excluded for his folly, before the son of his wise brother who reigned? Who has the *paternal power* whilst the widow-queen is with child by the deceased king, and no body knows whether it will be a son or a daughter? Which shall be heir of the two male-twins, who by the dissection of the mother were laid open to the world? Whether a sister by the half blood, before a brother's daughter by the whole blood?

§. 124. These, and many more such doubts, might be proposed about the titles of succession, and the right of inheritance; and that not as idle speculations, but such as in history we shall find have concerned the inheritance of crowns and kingdoms; and if our's want them, we need not go farther for famous examples of it, than the other kingdom in this very island, which having been fully related by the ingenious and learned author of *Patriarcha non Monarcha,* I need say no more of. Till our author hath resolved all the doubts that may arise about the next heir, and shewed that they are plainly determined by the law of nature, or the revealed law of God, all his suppositions of a *monarchical, absolute, supreme, paternal power* in *Adam,* and the descent of that power to his heirs, would not be of the least use to establish the authority, or make out the title, of any one prince now on earth; but would rather unsettle and bring all into question: for let our author tell us as long as he pleases, and let all men believe it too, that *Adam* had a *paternal,* and thereby a *monarchical power;* that this (the only *power* in the world) *descended to his heirs;* and that there is no other power in the world but this: let this be all as clear demonstration, as it is manifest error, yet if it be not past doubt, to whom this *paternal power descends,* and whose now it is, no body can be under any obligation of *obedience,* unless any one will say, that I am bound to pay obedience to *paternal power* in a man who has no more *paternal power* than I myself; which is all one as to say, I obey a man, because he has a right to govern; and if I be asked, how I know he has a right to govern, I should answer, it cannot be known, that he has any at all: for that cannot be the reason of my obedience, which I know not to be so; much less can that be a reason of my obedience, which no body at all can know to be so.

§. 125. And therefore all this ado about *Adam*'s *fatherhood,* the greatness of its power, and the necessity of its supposal, helps nothing to establish the power of those that govern, or to determine the obedience of subjects who are to obey, if they cannot tell whom they are to obey, or it cannot be known who are to govern, and who to obey. In the state the world is now, it is irrecoverably ignorant, who is *Adam*'s heir. This *fatherhood,* this *monarchical power of Adam,* descending to his heirs, would be of no more use to the government of mankind, than it would be to the quieting of mens consciences, or securing their healths, if our author had assured them, that *Adam* had a *power* to forgive sins, or cure diseases, which by divine institution descended to his *heir,* whilst this heir is impossible to be known. And should not he do as rationally, who upon this assurance of our author went and confessed his sins, and expected a good absolution; or took physic with expectation of health, from any one who had taken on himself the name of priest or physician, or thrust himself into those employments, saying, I acquiesce in the absolving power descending from *Adam,* or I shall be cured by the medicinal power descending from *Adam;* as he who says, I submit to and obey the *paternal power* descending from *Adam,* when it is confessed all these powers descend only to his single heir, and that heir is unknown?

§. 126. It is true, the civil lawyers have pretended to determine some of these cases concerning the succession of princes; but by our author's principles, they have meddled in a matter that belongs not to them: for if all political power be derived only from *Adam,* and be to descend only to his successive heirs, by the *ordinance of God* and *divine institution,* this is a right antecedent and paramount to all government; and therefore the positive laws of men cannot determine that, which is itself the foundation of all law and government, and is to receive its rule only from the law of God and nature. And that being silent in the case, I am apt to think there is no such right to be conveyed this way: I am sure it would be to no purpose if there were, and men would be more at a loss concerning government, and obedience to governors, than if there were no such right; since by positive laws and compact, which *divine institution* (if there be any) shuts out, all these endless inextricable doubts can be safely provided against: but it can never be understood, how a divine natural right, and that of such moment as is all order and peace in the world, should be conveyed down to posterity, without any plain natural or divine rule concerning it. And there would be an end of all civil government, if the *assignment* of civil power were by *divine institution* to the heir, and yet *by that divine institution* the person of the heir could not be known. This *paternal regal power* being by divine right only his, it leaves no room for human prudence, or consent, to place it any where else; for if only one man hath a divine right to the obedience of mankind, no body can claim that obedience, but he that can shew that right; nor can men's consciences by any other pretence be obliged to it. And thus this doctrine cuts up all government by the roots.

§. 127. Thus we see how our author, laying it for a sure foundation, that the very *person* that is to rule, is the *ordinance* of God, and by *divine institution,* tells us at large, only that this person is the *heir,* but who this heir is, he leaves us to guess; and so this *divine institution,* which assigns it to a person whom we have no rule to know, is just as good as an assignment to no body at all. But whatever our author does, *divine institution* makes no such ridiculous assignments: nor can God be supposed to make it a sacred law, that one certain person should have a right to something, and yet not give rules to mark out, and know that person by, or give an *heir* a divine right to power, and yet not point out who that *heir* is. It is rather to be thought, that an *heir* had no such right by *divine institution,* than that God should give such a right to the *heir,* but yet leave it doubtful and undeterminable who such heir is.

§. 128. If God had given the land of *Canaan* to *Abraham,* and in general terms to some body after him, without naming his seed, whereby it might be known who that somebody was, it would have been as good and useful an assignment, to determine the right to the land of *Canaan,* as it would be the determining the right of crowns, to give empire to *Adam* and his successive heirs after him, without telling who his heir is: for the word *heir,* without a rule to know who it is, signifies no more than some body, I know not whom. God making it a *divine institution,* that men should not marry those who were *near of kin,* thinks it not enough to say, *None of you shall approach to any that is near of kin to him, to uncover their nakedness;* but moreover, gives rules to know who are those *near of kin,* forbidden by *divine institution;* or else that law would have been of no use, it being to no purpose to lay restraint, or give privileges to men, in such general terms, as the particular person concerned cannot be known by. But God not having any where said, the next heir shall inherit all his father's estate or dominion, we are not to wonder, that he hath no where appointed who that heir should be; for never having intended any such thing, never designed any heir in that sense, we cannot expect he should any where nominate, or appoint any person to it, as we might, had it been otherwise. And therefore in scripture, though the word *heir* occur, yet there is no such thing as heir in our author's sense, one that was by right of nature to inherit all that his father had, exclusive of his brethren. Hence *Sarah* supposes, that if *Ishmael* staid in the house, to share in *Abraham*'s estate after his death, this son of a bond-woman might be heir with *Isaac;* and therefore, says she, *cast out this bond-woman and her son, for the son of this bond-woman shall not be heir with my son:* but this cannot excuse our author, who telling us there is, in every number of men, one who is right and next *heir* to *Adam,* ought to have told us what the laws of descent are: but he having been so sparing to instruct us by rules, how to know who is *heir,* let us see in the next place, what his history out of scripture, on which he pretends wholly to build his government, gives us in this necessary and fundamental point.

§. 129. Our author, to make good the title of his book, p. 13. begins his history of the descent of *Adam*'s regal power, p. 13. in these words: *This lordship which* Adam *by command had over the whole world, and by right descending from him, the patriarchs did enjoy, was a large,* &c. How does he prove that the patriarchs by descent did enjoy it? for *dominion of life and death,* says he, *we find* Judah *the father pronounced sentence of death against* Thamar *his daughter in law for playing the harlot,* p. 13. How does this prove that *Judah* had absolute and sovereign authority? *he pronounced sentence of death.* The pronouncing of sentence of death is not a certain mark of sovereignty, but usually the office of inferior magistrates. The power of making laws of life and death is indeed a mark of sovereignty, but pronouncing the sentence according to those laws may be done by others, and therefore this will but ill prove that he had sovereign authority: as if one should say, *Judge*

Jefferies pronounced sentence of death in the late times, therefore *Judge Jefferies* had sovereign authority. But it will be said, *Judah* did it not by commission from another, and therefore did it in his own right. Who knows whether he had any right at all? Heat of passion might carry him to do that which he had no authority to do. *Judah had dominion of life and death:* how does that appear? He exercised it, he *pronounced sentence of death against* Thamar: our author thinks it is very good proof, that because he did it, therefore he had a right to do it: he lay with her also: by the same way of proof, he had a right to do that too. If the consequence be good from doing to a right of doing, *Absalom* too may be reckoned amongst our author's sovereigns, for he pronounced such a sentence of death against his brother *Amnon,* and much upon a like occasion, and had it executed too, if that be sufficient to prove a dominion of life and death.

But allowing this all to be clear demonstration of sovereign power, who was it that had this *lordship by right descending to him from* Adam, *as large and ample as the absolutest dominion of any monarch? Judah,* says our author, *Judah* a younger son of *Jacob,* his father and elder brethren living; so that if our author's own proof be to be taken, a younger brother may, in the life of his father and elder brothers, *by right of descent, enjoy* Adam*'s monarchical power;* and if one so qualified may be monarch by descent, why may not every man? if *Judah,* his father and elder brother living, were one of *Adam*'s heirs, I know not who can be excluded from this inheritance; all men by inheritance may be monarchs as well as *Judah.*

§. 130. *Touching war, we see that* Abraham *commanded an army of* 318 *soldiers of his own family, and* Esau *met his brother* Jacob *with* 400 *men at arms: for matter of peace,* Abraham *made a league with* Abimelech, *&c.* p. 13. Is it not possible for a man to have 318 men in his family, without being heir to *Adam?* A planter in the *West Indies* has more, and might, if he pleased, (who doubts?) muster them up and lead them out against the *Indians,* to seek reparation upon any injury received from them; and all this without the *absolute dominion of a monarch, descending to him from* Adam. Would it not be an admirable argument to prove, that all power by God's institution descended from *Adam* by inheritance, and that the very person and power of this planter were the *ordinance of God,* because he had power in his family over servants, born in his house, and bought with his money? For this was just *Abraham*'s case; those who were rich in the *patriarch*'s days, as in the *West Indies* now, bought *men* and *maid servants,* and by their increase, as well as purchasing of new, came to have large and numerous families, which though they made use of in war or peace, can it be thought the power they had over them was an inheritance descended from *Adam,* when it was the purchase of their money? A man's riding in an expedition against an enemy, his horse bought in a fair would be as good a proof that the owner *enjoyed the lordship which* Adam *by* *command had over the whole world, by right descending to him,* as *Abraham*'s leading out the servants of his family is, that the *patriarchs* enjoyed this lordship by descent from *Adam:* since the title to the power, the master had in both cases, whether over slaves or horses, was only from his purchase; and the getting a dominion over any thing by bargain and money, is a new way of proving one had it by descent and inheritance.

§. 131. *But making war and peace are marks of sovereignty.* Let it be so in politic socities: may not therefore a man in the *West Indies,* who hath with him sons of his own, friends, or companions, soldiers under pay, or slaves bought with money, or perhaps a band made up of all these, make war and peace, if there should be occasion, and *ratify the articles too with an oath,* without being a sovereign, an absolute king over those who went with him? He that says he cannot, must then allow many masters of ships, many private planters, to be absolute monarchs, for as much as this they have done. War and peace cannot be made for politic societies, but by the supreme power of such societies; because war and peace, giving a different motion to the force of such a politic body, none can make war or peace, but that which has the direction of the force of the whole body, and that in politic societies is only the supreme power. In voluntary societies for the time, he that has such a power by consent, may make war and peace, and so may a single man for himself, the state of war not consisting in the number of *partisans,* but the enmity of the parties, where they have no superior to appeal to.

§. 132. The actual making of war or peace is no proof of any other power, but only of disposing those to exercise or cease acts of enmity for whom he makes it; and this power in many cases any one may have without any politic supremacy: and therefore the making of war or peace will not prove that every one that does so is a politic ruler, much less a king; for then common-wealths must be kings too, for they do as certainly make war and peace as monarchical government.

§. 133. But granting this a *mark of sovereignty* in *Abraham,* is it a proof of the descent to him of *Adam's sovereignty* over the whole world? If it be, it will surely be as good a proof of the *descent of* Adam'*s lordship* to others too. And then common-wealths, as well as *Abraham,* will be *heirs of Adam,* for they make *war and peace,* as well as he. If you say, that the *lordship of Adam* doth not by right descend to common-wealths, though they make war and peace, the same say I of *Abraham,* and then there is an end of your argument: if you stand to your argument, and say those that do make war and peace, as common-wealths do without doubt, do *inherit* Adam'*s lordship,* there is an end of your monarchy, unless you will say, that commonwealths *by descent enjoying* Adam'*s lordship* are monarchies; and that indeed would be a new way of making all the governments in the world monarchical.

§. 134. To give our author the honour of this new invention, for I confess it is not I have first found it out by tracing his principles, and so charged it on him, it is fit my readers know that (as absurd as it may seem) he teaches it himself, p. 23. where he ingenuously says, *In all kingdoms and common-wealths in the world, whether the prince be the supreme father of the people, or but the true heir to such a father, or come to the crown by usurpation or election, or whether some few or a multitude govern the common-wealth; yet still the authority that is in any one, or in many, or in all these, is the only right, and natural authority of a supreme father;* which right of *fatherhood,* he often tells us, is *regal and royal authority;* as particularly, p. 12. the page immediately preceding this instance of *Abraham.* This regal authority, he says, those that govern common-wealths have; and if it be true, that regal and royal authority be in those that govern common-wealths, it is as true that common-wealths are governed by kings; for if regal authority be in him that governs, he that governs must needs be a king, and so all common-wealths are nothing but down-right monarchies; and then what need any more ado about the matter? The governments of the world are as they should be, there is nothing but monarchy in it. This, without doubt, was the surest way our author could have found, to turn all other governments, but monarchical, out of the world.

§. 135. But all this scarce proves *Abraham* to have been a king as heir to *Adam.* If by inheritance he had been king, *Lot,* who was of the same family, must needs have been his subject, by that title, before the servants in his family; but we see they lived as friends and equals, and when their herdsmen could not agree, there was no pretence of jurisdiction or superiority between them, but they parted by consent, *Gen.* xiii. hence he is called both by *Abraham,* and by the text, *Abraham's brother,* the name of friendship and equality, and not of jurisdiction and authority, though he were really but his nephew. And if our author knows that *Abraham* was *Adam*'s heir, and a king, it was more, it seems, than *Abraham* himself knew, or his servant whom he sent a wooing for his son; for when he sets out the advantages of the match, xxiv. *Gen.* 35. thereby to prevail with the young woman and her friends, he says, *I am Abraham's servant, and the lord hath blessed my master greatly, and he is become great; and he hath given him flocks and herds, and silver and gold, and men-servants and maid-servants, and camels and asses; and Sarah, my master's wife, bare a son to my master when she was old, and unto him hath he given all he hath.* Can one think that a discreet servant, that was thus particular to set out his master's greatness, would have omitted the crown *Isaac* was to have, if he had known of any such? Can it be imagined he should have neglected to have told them on such an occasion as this, that *Abraham* was a king, a name well known at that time, for he had nine of them his neighbours, if he or his master had thought any such thing, the likeliest matter of all the rest, to make his errand successful?

§. 136. But this discovery it seems was reserved for our author to make 2 or 3000 years after, and let him enjoy the credit of it; only he should have taken care that some of *Adam*'s land should have descended to this his *heir,* as well as all *Adam*'s lordship: for though this lordship which *Abraham,* (if we may believe our author) as well as the other patriarchs, *by right descending to him, did enjoy, was as large and ample as the absolutest dominion of any monarch which hath been since the creation;* yet his estate, his territories, his dominions were very narrow and scanty, for he had not the possession of a foot of land, till he bought a field and a cave of the sons of *Heth* to bury *Sarah* in.

§. 137. The instance of *Esau* joined with this of *Abraham,* to prove that the *lordship which* Adam *had over the whole world, by right descending from him, the patriarchs did enjoy,* is yet more pleasant than the former. *Esau met his brother* Jacob *with* 400 *men at arms;* he therefore was a king by right of heir to *Adam.* Four hundred armed men then, however got together, are enough to prove him that leads them, to be a king and *Adam*'s heir. There have been tories in *Ireland,* (whatever there are in other countries) who would have thanked our author for so honourable an opinion of them, especially if there had been no body near with a better title of 500 armed men, to question their royal authority of 400. It is a shame for men to trifle so, to say no worse of it, in so serious an argument. Here *Esau* is brought as a proof that *Adam*'s lordship, *Adam's absolute dominion, as large as that of any monarch, descended by right to the patriarchs,* and in this very *chap.* p. 19. *Jacob* is brought as an instance of one, that by *birth-right was lord over his brethren.* So we have here two brothers absolute monarchs by the same title, and at the same time heirs to *Adam;* the eldest, heir to *Adam,* because he met his brother with 400 men; and the youngest, heir to *Adam* by *birth-right:* Esau *enjoyed the lordship which* Adam *had over the whole world by right descending to him, in as large and ample manner, as the absolutest dominion of any monarch;* and at the same time, *Jacob lord over him, by the right heirs have to be lords over their brethren. Risum teneatis?* I never, I confess, met with any man of parts so dexterous as Sir *Robert* at this way of arguing: but it was his misfortune to light upon an *hypothesis,* that could not be accommodated to the nature of things, and human affairs; his principles could not be made to agree with that constitution and order, which God had settled in the world, and therefore must needs often clash with common sense and experience.

§. 138. In the next section, he tells us, *This patriarchal power continued not only till the flood, but after it, as the name patriarch doth in part prove.* The word patriarch doth more than *in part prove,* that *patriarchal power* continued in the world as long as there were patriarchs, for it is necessary that patriarchal power should be whilst there are patriarchs; as it is necessary there should be paternal or conjugal power whilst there are fathers or husbands; but this is but playing with names. That which he would fallaciously insinuate is the thing in question to be proved, *viz.* that the *lordship which* Adam *had over the world,* the supposed absolute universal dominion of *Adam* by *right descending from him, the patriarchs did enjoy.* If he affirms such an absolute monarchy continued to the flood, in the world, I would be glad to know what records he has it from; for I confess I cannot find a word of it in my Bible: if by *patriarchal power* he means any thing else, it is nothing to the matter in hand. And how the name *patriarch* in some part proves, that those, who are called by that name, had absolute monarchical power, I confess, I do not see, and therefore I think needs no answer till the argument from it be made out a little clearer.

§. 139. *The three sons of* Noah *had the world, says our author, divided amongst them by their father, for of them was the whole world overspread,* p. 14. The world might be overspread by the offspring of *Noah*'s sons, though he never divided the world amongst them; for the earth might be replenished without being divided: so that all our author's argument here proves no such division. However, I allow it to him, and then ask, the world being divided amongst them, which of the three was *Adam*'s heir? If *Adam's lordship, Adam's monarchy,* by right descended only to the eldest, then the other two could be but his *subjects,* his *slaves:* if by right it descended to all three brothers, by the same right, it will descend to all mankind; and then it will be impossible what he says, p. 19. that *heirs are lords of their brethren,* should be true; but all brothers, and consequently all men, will be equal and independent, all heirs to *Adam*'s monarchy, and consequently all monarchs too, one as much as another. But it will be said, *Noah* their father divided the world amongst them; so that our author will allow more to *Noah,* than he will to God almighty, for *Observations,* 211. he thought it hard, that God himself should give the world to *Noah* and his sons, to the prejudice of *Noah*'s birth-right: his words are, *Noah was left sole heir to the world: why should it be thought that God would disinherit him of his birth-right, and make him, of all men in the world, the only tenant in common with his children?* and yet here he thinks it fit that *Noah* should disinherit *Shem* of his birth-right, and divide the world betwixt him and his brethren; so that this *birth-right,* when our author pleases, must, and when he pleases must not, be sacred and inviolable.

§. 140. If *Noah* did divide the world between his sons, and his assignment of dominions to them were good, there is an end of divine institution; all our author's discourse of *Adam*'s heir, with whatsoever he builds on it, is quite out of doors; the natural power of kings falls to the ground; and then *the form of the power governing, and the person having that power, will not be* (as he says they are, *Observations,* 254.) *the ordinance of God,* but they will be *ordinances of man:* for if the right of the heir be the ordinance of God, a divine right, no man, father or not father, can alter it: if it be not a divine right, it is only human, depending on the will of man: and so where human institution gives it not, the first-born has no right at all above his brethren; and men may put government into what hands, and under what form, they please.

§. 141. He goes on, *Most of the civilest nations of the earth labour to fetch their originalfrom some of the sons, or nephews of* Noah, p. 14. How many do most of the civilest nations amount to? and who are they? I fear the *Chineses,* a very great and civil people, as well as several other people of the *East, West, North* and *South,* trouble not themselves much about this matter. All that believe the Bible, which I believe are our author's *most of the civilest nations,* must necessarily derive themselves from *Noah;* but for the rest of the world, they think little of his sons or nephews. But if the heralds and antiquaries of all nations, for it is these men generally that labour to find out the originals of nations, or all the nations themselves, *should labour to fetch their original from some of the sons or nephews of* Noah, what would this be to prove, that the *lordship which* Adam *had over the whole world, by right descended to the patriarchs?* Whoever, nations, or races of men, *labour to fetch their original from,* may be concluded to be thought by them, men of renown, famous to posterity, for the greatness of their virtues and actions; but beyond these they look not, nor consider who they were heirs to, but look on them as such as raised themselves, by their own virtue, to a degree that would give a lustre to those who in future ages could pretend to derive themselves from them. But if it were *Ogyges, Hercules, Brama, Tamberlain, Pharamond;* nay, if *Jupiter* and *Saturn* were the names, from whence divers races of men, both ancient and modern, have laboured to derive their original; will that prove, that those men *enjoyed the lordship of* Adam, *by right descending to them?* If not, this is but a flourish of our author's to mislead his reader, that in itself signifies nothing.

§. 142. To as much purpose is what he tells us, p. 15. concerning this division of the world, *That some say it was by* Lot, *and others that* Noah *sailed round the* Mediterreanean *in ten years, and divided the world into* Asia, Afric *and* Europe, portions for his three sons. *America* then, it seems, was left to be his that could catch it. Why our author takes such pains to prove the division of the world by *Noah* to his sons, and will not leave out an imagination, though no better than a dream, that he can find any where to favour it, is hard to guess, since such a *division,* if it prove any thing, must necessarily take away the title of *Adam*'s heir; unless three brothers can all together be heirs of *Adam;* and therefore the following words, *Howsoever the manner of this division be uncertain, yet it is most certain the division itself was by families from* Noah *and his children, over which the parents were heads and princes,* p. 15. if allowed him to be true, and of any sorce to prove, that all the power in the world is nothing but the lordship *of* Adam'*s descending by right,* they will only prove, that the fathers of the children are all heirs to this lordship of *Adam:* for if in those days *Cham* and *Japhet,* and other parents, besides the eldest son, were heads and princes over their families, and had a right to divide the earth by families, what hinders younger brothers, being fathers of families, from having the same right? If *Cham* and *Japhet* were princes by right descending to them, notwithstanding any title of heir in their eldest brother, younger brothers by the same right descending to them are princes now; and so all our author's natural power of kings will reach no farther than their own children, and no kingdom, by this natural right, can be bigger than a family: for either this *lordship of* Adam *over the whole world,* by right descends only to the eldest son, and then there can be but one heir, as our author says, p. 19. or else, it by right descends to all the sons equally, and then every father of a family will have it, as well as the three sons of *Noah:* take which you will, it destroys the present governments and kingdoms, that are now in the world, since whoever has this *natural power of a king,* by right descending to him, must have it, either as our author tells us *Cain* had it, and be lord over his brethren, and so be alone king of the whole world; or else, as he tells us here, *Shem, Cham* and *Japhet* had it, three brothers, and so be only prince of his own family, and all families independent one of another: all the world must be only one empire by the right of the next heir, or else every family be a distinct government of itself, by the *lordship of* Adam'*s descending to parents of families.* And to this only tend all the proofs he here gives us of the descent of *Adam*'s lordship: for continuing his story of this descent, he says,

§. 143. *In the dispersion of* Babel, *we must certainly find the establishment of royal power, throughout the kingdoms of the world,* p. 14. If you must find it, pray do, and you will help us to a new piece of history: but you must shew it us before we shall be bound to believe, that regal power was established in the world upon your principles: for, that regal power was established *in the kingdoms of the world,* I think no body will dispute; but that there should be kingdoms in the world, whose several kings enjoyed their crowns, *by right descending to them from* Adam, that we think not only *apocryphal,* but also utterly impossible. If our author has no better foundation for his monarchy than a supposition of what was done at the dispersion of *Babel,* the monarchy he erects thereon, whose top is to reach to heaven to unite mankind, will serve only to divide and scatter them as that tower did; and, instead of establishing civil government and order in the world, will produce nothing but confusion.

§. 144. For he tells us, the *nations* they were divided into, *were distinct families, which had fathers for rulers over them; whereby it appears, that even in the confusion, God was careful to preserve the fatherly authority, by distributing the diversity of languages according to the diversity of families,* p. 14. It would have been a hard matter for any one but our author to have found out so plainly, in the text he here brings, that all the nations in that dispersion were governed by *fathers,* and that *God was careful to preserve the fatherly authority.* The words of the text are; *These are the sons of Shem after their families, after their tongues in their lands, after their nations;* and the same thing is said of *Cham* and *Japhet,* after an enumeration of their posterities; in all which there is not one word said of their governors, or forms of government; of *fathers,* or *fatherly authority.* But our author, who is very quick sighted to spy out *fatherhood,* where no body else could see any the least glimpses of it, tells us positively their *rulers were fathers, and God was careful to preserve the fatherly authority;* and why? Because those of the same family spoke the same language, and so of necessity in the division kept together. Just as if one should argue thus: *Hanibal* in his army, consisting of divers nations, kept those of the same language together; therefore fathers were captains of each band, and *Hanibal* was careful of the *fatherly authority:* or in peopling of *Carolina,* the *English, French, Scotch* and *Welch* that are there, plant themselves together, and by them the country is divided *in their lands after their tongues, after their families, after their nations;* therefore care was taken of the *fatherly authority:* or because, in many parts of *America,* every little tribe was a distinct people, with a different language, one should infer, that therefore *God was careful to preserve the fatherly authority,* or that therefore their rulers *enjoyed* Adam'*s lordship by right descending to them,* though we know not who were their governors, nor what their form of government, but only that they were divided into little independent societies, speaking different languages.

§. 145. The scripture says not a word of their rulers or forms of government, but only gives an account, how mankind came to be divided into distinct languages and nations; and therefore it is not to argue from the authority of scripture, to tell us positively, *fathers* were their *rulers,* when the scripture says no such thing; but to set up fancies of one's own brain, when we confidently aver matter of fact, where records are utterly silent. Upon a like ground, *i. e.* none at all, he says, *That they were not confused multitudes without heads and governors, and at liberty to choose what governors or governments they pleased.*

§. 146. For I demand, when mankind were all yet of one language, all congregated in the plain of *Shinar,* were they then all under one monarch, *who enjoyed the lordship of* Adam *by right descending to him?* If they were not, there were then no thoughts, it is plain, of *Adam*'s *heir,* no right to government known then upon that title; no care taken, by God or man, of *Adam*'s *fatherly authority.* If when mankind were but one people, dwelt all together, and were of one language, and were upon building a city together; and when it was plain, they could not but know the right heir, for *Shem* lived till *Isaac*'s time, a long while after the division at *Babel;* if then, I say, they were not under the monarchical government of *Adam*'s fatherhood, by right descending to the heir, it is plain there was no regard had to the *fatherhood,* no monarchy acknowledged due to *Adam*'s *heir,* no empire of *Shem*'s in *Asia,* and consequently no such division of the world by *Noah,* as our author has talked of. As far as we can conclude any thing from scripture in this matter, it seems from this place, that if they had any government, it was rather a commonwealth than an absolute monarchy: for the scripture tells us, *Gen.* xi. *They said:* it was not a prince commanded the building of this city and tower, it was not by the command of one *monarch,* but by the consultation of many, a free people; *let us buildus a city:* they built it for themselves as free-men, not as slaves for their lord and master: *that we be not scattered abroad;* having a city once built, and fixed habitations to settle our abodes and families. This was the consultation and design of a people, that were at liberty to part asunder, but desired to keep in one body, and could not have been either necessary or likely in men tied together under the government of one monarch, who if they had been, as our author tells us, all *slaves* under the absolute dominion of a monarch, needed not have taken such care to hinder themselves from wandering out of the reach of his dominion. I demand whether this be not plainer in scripture than any thing of *Adam*'s *heir or fatherly authority?*

§. 147. But if being, as God says, *Gen.* xi. 6. one people, they had one ruler, one king by natural right, absolute and supreme over them, *what care had God to preserve the paternal authority of the supreme fatherhood,* if on a sudden he suffer 72 (for so many our author talks of) *distinct nations* to be erected out of it, under distinct governors,·and at once to withdraw themselves from the obedience of their sovereign? This is to intitle God's care how, and to what we please. Can it be sense to say, that God was careful to preserve the *fatherly authority* in those who had it not? for if these were subjects under a supreme prince, what authority had they? Was it an instance of God's care to preserve the *fatherly authority,* when he took away the true *supreme fatherhood* of the natural monarch? Can it be reason to say, that God, for the preservation of *fatherly authority,* lets several new governments with their governors start up, who could not all have *fatherly authority?* And is it not as much reason to say, that God is careful to destroy *fatherly authority,* when he suffers one, who is in possession of it, to have his government torn in pieces, and shared by several of his subjects? Would it not be an argument just like this, for monarchical government, to say, when any monarchy was shattered to pieces, and divided amongst revolted subjects, that God was careful to preserve monarchical power, by rending a settled empire into a multitude of little governments? If any one will say, that what happens in providence to be preserved, God is careful to preserve as a thing therefore to be esteemed by men as necessary or useful, it is a peculiar propriety of speech, which every one will not think fit to imitate: but this I am sure is impossible to be either proper, or true speaking, that *Shem,* for example, (for he was then alive,) should have *fatherly authority,* or sovereignty by right of *fatherhood,* over that one people at *Babel,* and that the next moment, *Shem* yet living, 72 others should have *fatherly authority,* or sovereignty by right of fatherhood, over the same people, divided into so many distinct governments: either these 72 fathers actually were rulers, just before the confusion, and then they were not one people, but that God himself says they were; or else they were a commonwealth, and then where was monarchy? or else these 72 fathers had *fatherly authority,* but knew it not. Strange! that *fatherly authority* should be the only original of government amongst men, and yet all mankind not know it; and stranger yet, that the confusion of tongues should reveal it to them all of a sudden, that in an instant these 72 should know that they had *fatherly power,* and all others know that they were to obey it in them, and every one know that particular *fatherly authority* to which he was a subject. He that can think this arguing from scripture, may from thence make out what model of an *Eutopia* will best suit with his fancy or interest; and this *fatherhood,* thus disposed of, will justify both a prince who claims an universal monarchy, and his subjects, who, being fathers of families, shall quit all subjection to him, and *canton* his empire into less governments for themselves; for it will always remain a doubt in which of these the fatherly authority resided, till our author resolves us, whether *Shem,* who was then alive, or these 72 new princes, beginning so many new empires in his dominions, and over his subjects, had right to govern, since our author tells us, that both one and the other had *fatherly,* which is supreme authority, and are brought in by him as instances of those who did *enjoy the lordships of* Adam *by right descending to them, which was as large and ample as the absolutest dominion of any monarch.* This at least is unavoidable, that if *God was careful to preserve the fatherly authority, in the 72 new-erected nations,* it necessarily follows, that he was as careful to destroy all pretences of *Adam*'s heir; fince he took care, and therefore did preserve the fatherly authority in so many, at least 71, that could not possibly be *Adam*'s heirs, when the right heir (if God had ever ordained any such inheritance) could not but be known, *Shem* then living, and they being all one people.

§. 148. *Nimrod* is his next instance of enjoying this patriarchal power, p. 16. but I know not for what reason our author seems a little unkind to him, and says, that he *against right enlarged his empire, by seizing violently on the rights of other lords of families.* These *lords of families* here were called *fathers of families,* in his account of the dispersion at *Babel:* but it matters not how they were called, so we know who they are; for this fatherly authority must be in them, either as heirs to *Adam,* and so there could not be 72, nor above one at once; or else as natural parents over their children, and so every father will have *paternal authority* over his children by the same right, and in as large extent as those 72 had, and so be independent princes over their own offspring. Taking his *lords of families* in this later sense, (as it is hard to give those words any other sense in this place) he gives us a very pretty account of the original of monarchy, in these following words, p. 16. *And in this sense he may be said to be the author and founder of monarchy,* viz. As against right seizing violently on the rights of fathers over their children; which paternal authority, if it be in them, by right of nature, (for else how could those 72 come by it?) no body can take from them without their own consents; and then I desire our author and his friends to consider, how far this will concern other princes, and whether it will not, according to his conclusion of that paragraph, resolve all regal power of those, whose dominions extend beyond their families, either into tyranny and usurpation, or election and consent of fathers of families, which will differ very little from consent of the people.

§. 149. All his instances, in the next *section,* p. 17. of the 12 dukes of *Edom,* the nine kings in a little corner of *Asia* in *Abraham*'s days, the 31 kings in *Canaan* destroyed by *Joshua,* and the care he takes to prove that these were all sovereign princes, and that every town in those days had a king, are so many direct proofs against him, that it was not the *lordship of* Adam *by right descending* to them, that made kings: for if they had held their royalties by that title, either there must have been but one sovereign over them all, or else every father of a family had been as good a prince, and had as good a claim to royalty, as these: for if all the sons of *Esau* had each of them, the younger as well as the eldest, the right of *fatherhood,* and so were sovereign princes after their fathers death, the same right had their sons after them, and so on to all posterity; which will limit all the natural power of fatherhood, only to be over the issue of their own bodies, and their descendents; which power of fatherhood dies with the head of each family, and makes way for the like power of fatherhood to take place in each of his sons over their respective posterities: whereby the power of fatherhood will be preserved indeed, and is intelligible, but will not be at all to our author's purpose. None of the instances he brings are proofs of any power they had, as heirs of *Adam*'s paternal authority by the title of his fatherhood descending to them; no, nor of any power they had by virtue of their own: for *Adam*'s *fatherhood* being over all mankind, it could descend but to one at once, and from him to his right heir only, and so there could by that title be but one king in the world at a time: and by right of fatherhood, not descending from *Adam,* it must be only as they themselves were fathers, and so could be over none but their own posterity. So that if those 12 dukes of *Edom;* if *Abraham* and the nine kings his neighbours; if *Jacob* and *Esau,* and the 31 kings in *Canaan,* the 72 kings mutilated by *Adonibeseck,* the 32 kings that came to *Benhadad,* the 70 kings of *Greece* making war at *Troy,* were, as our author contends, all of them sovereign princes; it is evident that kings derived their power from some other original *than fatherhood,* since some of these had power over more than their own posterity; and it is demonstration, they could not be all heirs to *Adam:* for I challenge any man to make any pretence to power by right of *fatherhood,* either intelligible or possible in any one, otherwise, than either as *Adam*'s heir, or as progenitor over his own descendents, naturally sprung from him. And if our author could shew that any one of these princes, of which he gives us here so large a catalogue, had his authority by either of these titles, I think I might yield him the cause; though it is manifest they are all impertinent, and directly contrary to what he brings them to prove, *viz.* That the *lordship which* Adam *had over the world by right descended to the patriarchs.*

§. 150. Having told us, p. 16, That *the patriarchal government continued in* Abraham, Isaac, *and* Jacob, *until the* Egyptian *bondage,* p. 17. he tells us, *By manifest footsteps we may trace this paternal government unto the* Israelites *coming into* Egypt, *where the exercise of supreme patriarchal government was intermitted, because they were in subjection to a stronger prince.* What these footsteps are of paternal government, in our author's sense, *i. e.* of absolute monarchical power descending from *Adam,* and exercised by right of *fatherhood,* we have seen, that is for 2290 years no footsteps at all; since in all that time he cannot produce any one example of any person who claimed or exercised regal authority by right of *fatherhood;* or shew any one who being a king was *Adam*'s heir: all that his proofs amount to, is only this, that there were fathers, patriarchs and kings, in that age of the world; but that the fathers and patriarchs had any absolute arbitrary power, or by what titles those kings had their's, and of what extent it was, the scripture is wholly filent; it is manifest by right of *fatherhood* they neither did, nor could claim any title to dominion and empire.

§. 151. To say, *that the exercise of supreme patriarchal government was intermitted, because they were in subjection to a stronger prince,* proves nothing but what I before suspected, *viz.* That *patriarchal jurisdiction or government* is a fallacious expression, and does not in our author signify (what he would yet insinuate by it) *paternal* and *regal power,* such an absolute sovereignty as he supposes was in *Adam.*

§. 152. For how can he say that *patriarchal jurisdiction was intermitted in Egypt,* where there was a king, under whose regal government the *Israelites* were, if *patriarchal* were *absolute monarchical jurisdiction?* And if it were not, but something else, why does he make such ado about a power not in question, and nothing to the purpose? The exercise of *patriarchal* jurisdiction, if *patriarchal* be *regal,* was not intermitted whilst the *Israelites* were in *Egypt.* It is true, the exercise of *regal* power was not then in the hands of any of the promised seed of *Abraham,* nor before neither that I know; but what is that to the intermission of *regal authority, as descending from* Adam, unless our author will have it, that this chosen line of *Abraham* had the right of inheritance to *Adam*'s lordship? and then to what purpose are his instances of the 72 rulers, in whom the fatherly authority was preserved in the confusion at *Babel?* Why does he bring the 12 princes sons of *Ismael;* and the dukes of *Edom,* and join them with *Abraham, Isaac,* and *Jacob,* as examples of the exercise of true *patriarchal government,* if the exercise of *patriarchal jurisdiction* were intermitted in the world, whenever the heirs of *Jacob* had not supreme power? I fear, *supreme patriarchal jurisdiction* was not only *intermitted,* but from the time of the *Egyptian* bondage quite lost in the world, since it will be hard to find, from that time downwards, any one who exercised it as an inheritance descending to him from the patriarchs *Abraham, Isaac,* and *Jacob.* I imagined monarchical government would have served his turn in the hands of *Pharaoh,* or any body. But one cannot easily discover in all places what his discourse tends to, as particularly in this place it is not obvious to guess what he drives at, when he says, *the exercise of supreme patriarchal jurisdiction* in *Egypt,* or how this serves to make out the descent of *Adam*'s lordship to the patriarchs, or any body else.

§. 153. For I thought he had been giving us out of scripture, proofs and examples of monarchical government, founded on paternal authority, descending from *Adam;* and not an history of the *Jews:* amongst whom yet we find no kings, till many years after they were a people: and when kings were their rulers, there is not the least mention or room for a pretence that they were heirs to *Adam,* or kings by paternal authority. I expected, talking so much as he does of scripture, that he would have produced thence a series of monarchs, whose titles were clear to *Adam's fatherhood,* and who, as heirs to him, owned and exercised paternal jurisdiction over their subjects, and that this was the true patriarchical government; whereas he neither proves, that the patriarchs were kings; nor that either kings or patriarchs were heirs to *Adam,* or so much as pretended to it: and one may as well prove, that the patriarchs were all absolute monarchs; that the power both of patriarchs and kings was only paternal; and that this power descended to them from *Adam:* I say all these propositions may be as well proved by a confused account of a multitude of little kings in the *West-Indies,* out of *Ferdinando Soto,* or any of our late histories of the *Northern America,* or by our author's 70 kings of *Greece,* out of *Homer,* as by any thing he brings out of scripture, in that multitude of kings he has reckoned up.

§. 154. And methinks he should have let *Homer* and his wars of *Troy* alone, since his great zeal to truth or monarchy carried him to such a pitch of transport against *philosophers* and *poets,* that he tells us in his preface, that there *are too many in these days, who please themselves in running after the opinions of philosophers and poets, to find out such an original of government, as might promise them some title to liberty, to the great scandal of Christianity, and bringing in of atheism.* And yet these heathens, philosopher *Aristotle,* and poet *Homer,* are not rejected by our zealous Christian politician, whenever they offer any thing that seems to serve his turn; whether *to the great scandal of* Christianity *and bringing in of* atheism, let him look. This I cannot but observe, in authors who it is visible write not for truth, how ready zeal for interest and party is to entitle *Christianity* to their designs, and to charge *atheism* on those who will not without examining submit to their doctrines, and blindly swallow their nonsense.

But to return to his scripture history, our author farther tells us, p. 18. that *after the return of the* Israelites *out of* bondage, *God, out of a special care of them, chose* Moses *and* Joshua *successively to govern as princes in the place and stead of the supreme fathers.* If it be true, that they *returned out of bondage,* it must be into a state of freedom, and must imply, that both before and after this *bondage* they were free, unless our author will say, that changing of masters is returning *out of bondage;* or that a slave *returns out of bondage,* when he is removed from one gally to another. If then they *returned out of bondage,* it is plain that in those days, whatever our author in his preface says to the contrary, there were difference between a *son,* a *subject,* and a *slave;* and that neither the *patriarchs* before, nor their rulers after this *Egyptian bondage, numbered their sons or subjects amongst their possessions,* and disposed of them with as absolute a dominion, as they did *their other goods.*

§. 155. This is evident in *Jacob,* to whom *Reuben* offered his two sons as pledges; and *Judah* was at last surety for *Benjamin*'s safe return out of *Egypt:* which all had been vain, superfluous, and but a sort of mockery, if *Jacob* had had the same power over every one of his family, as he had over his ox or his ass, as an *owner* over his *substance;* and the offers that *Reuben* or *Judah* made had been such a security for returning of *Benjamin,* as if a man should take two lambs out of his lord's flock, and offer one as security, that he will safely restore the other.

§. 156. When they were out of this *bondage,* what then? *God out of a special care of them, the* Israelites. It is well that once in his book he will allow God to have any care of the people; for in other places he speaks of mankind, as if God had no care of any part of them, but only of their monarchs, and that the rest of the people, the societies of men, were made as so many herds of cattle, only for the service, use, and pleasure of their princes.

§. 157. *Chose* Moses *and* Joshua *successively to govern as princes;* a shrewd argument our author has found out to prove God's care of the fatherly authority, and *Adam*'s heirs, that here, as an expression of his care of his own people, he chooses those for princes over them, that had not the least pretence to either. The persons chosen were, *Moses* of the tribe of *Levi,* and *Joshua* of the tribe of *Ephraim,* neither of which had any title of *fatherhood.* But says our author, they were in the place and stead of the supreme fathers. If God had any where as plainly declared his choice of such *fathers* to be rulers, as he did of *Moses* and *Joshua,* we might believe *Mases* and *Joshua* were in *their place and stead:* but that being the question in debate, till that be better proved, *Moses* being chosen by God to be ruler of his people, will no more prove that government belonged to *Adam's heir,* or to the *fatherhood,* than God's choosing *Aaron* of the tribe of *Levi* to be priest, will prove that the priesthood belonged to *Adam*'s heir, or the *prime fathers;* since God would choose *Aaron* to be priest, and *Moses* ruler in *Israel,* though neither of those offices were settled on *Adam*'s *heir,* or the *fatherhood.*

§. 158. Our author goes on, *and after them likewise for a time he raised up judges, to defend his people in time of peril,* p. 18. This proves fatherly authority to be the original of government, and that it descended from *Adam* to his heirs, just as well as what went before: only here our author seems to confess, that these judges, who were all the governors they then had, were only men of valour, whom they made their generals to defend them in time of peril; and cannot God raise up such men, unless fatherhood have a title to government?

But says our author, *when God gave the* Israelites *kings, he re-established the ancient andprime right of lineal succession to paternal government,* p. 18.

§. 160. How did God *re-establish* it? by a law, a positive command? We find no such thing. Our author means then, that when God gave them a king, in giving them a king, he *re-established the right, &c.* To re-establish *de facto* the right of lineal succession to paternal government, is to put a man in possession of that government which his fathers did enjoy, and he by lineal succession had a right to: for, first, if it were another government than what his ancestors had, it was not succeeding to an *ancient right,* but beginning a new one: for if a prince should give a man, besides his antient patrimony, which for some ages his family had been disseized of, an additional estate, never before in the possession of his ancestors, he could not be said to *re-establish the right of lineal succession* to any more than what had been formerly enjoyed by his ancestors. If therefore the power the kings of *Israel* had, were any thing more than *Isaac* or *Jacob* had, it was not the *re-establishing* in them the right of succession to a power, but giving them a new power, however you please to call it, *paternal* or not: and whether *Isaac* and *Jacob* had the same power that the kings of *Israel* had, I desire any one, by what has been above said, to consider; and I do not think they will find, that either *Abraham, Isaac,* or *Jacob,* had any regal power at all.

§. 161. Next, there can be no *re-establishment of the prime and ancient right of lineal succession* to any thing, unless he, that is put in possession of it, has the right to succeed, and be the true and next heir to him he succeeds to. Can that be a re-establishment, which begins in a new family? or that the *re-establishment of an ancient right of lineal succession,* when a crown is given to one, who has no right of succession to it, and who, if the lineal succession had gone on, had been out of all possibility of pretence to it? *Saul,* the first king God gave the *Israelites,* was of the tribe of *Benjamin.* Was the *ancient and prime right of lineal succession re-established* in him? The next was *David,* the youngest son of *Jesse,* of the posterity of *Judah, Jacob's third son.* Was the *ancient and prime right of lineal succession to paternal government re-established* in him? or in *Solomon,* his younger son and successor in the throne? or in *Jereboam* over the ten tribes? or in *Athaliah,* a woman who reigned six years an utter stranger to the royal blood? *If the ancient and prime right of lineal succession to paternal government* were *re-established* in any of these or their posterity, *the ancient and prime right of lineal succession to paternal government* belongs to younger brothers as well as elder, and may be re-established in any man living; for whatever younger brothers, by *ancient and prime right of lineal succession,* may have as well as the elder, that every man living may have a right to, by lineal succession, and Sir *Robert* as well as any other. And so what a brave right of lineal succession, to his *paternal* or *regal* government, our author has *re-established,* for the securing the rights and inheritance of crowns, where every one may have it, let the world consider.

§. 162. But says our author however, p. 19. *Whensoever God made choice of any special person to be king, he intended that the issue also should have benefit thereof, as being comprehended sufficiently in the person of the father, altho' the father was only named in the grant.* This yet will not help out succession; for if, as our author says, the benefit of the grant be intended to the *issue* of the grantee, this will not direct the succession; since, if God give any thing to a man and his *issue* in general, the claim cannot be to any one of that *issue* in particular; every one that is of his race will have an equal right. If it be said, our author meant *heir,* I believe our author was as willing as any body to have used that word, if it would have served his turn: but *Solomon,* who succeeded *David* in the throne, being no more his heir than *Jeroboham,* who succeeded him in the government of the ten tribes, was his issue, our author had reason to avoid saying, That God intended it to the *heirs,* when that would not hold in a succession, which our author could not except against; and so he has left his succession as undetermined, as if he had said nothing about it: for if the regal power be given by God to a man and his *issue,* as the land of *Canaan* was to *Abraham* and his seed, must they not all have a title to it, all share in it? And one may as well say, that by God's grant to *Abraham* and his seed, the land of *Canaan* was to belong only to one of his seed exclusive of all others, as by God's grant of dominion to a man and *his issue,* this dominion was to belong in peculiar to one of his *issue* exclusive of all others.

§. 163. But how will our author prove that whensoever God made choice of any special person to be a king, he intended that *the* (I suppose he means his) *issue also should have benefit thereof?* has he so soon forgot *Moses* and *Joshua,* whom in this very *section,* he says, *God out of a special care chose to govern as princes,* and the judges that God raised up? Had not these princes, having the authority of the *supreme fatherhood,* the same power that the kings had; and being specially chosen by God himself, should not their *issue* have the benefit of that choice, as well as *David*'s or *Solomon*'s? If these had the paternal authority put into their hands immediately by God, why had not their *issue* the benefit of this grant in a succession to this power? or if they had it as *Adam*'s heirs, why did not their heirs enjoy it after them by right descending to them? for they could not be heirs to one another. Was the power the same, and from the same original, in *Moses, Joshua* and the *Judges,* as it was in *David* and the *Kings;* and was it inheritable in one, and not in the other? If it was not *paternal authority,* then God's own people were governed by those that had not *paternal authority,* and those governors did well enough without it: if it were *paternal authority,* and God chose the persons that were to exercise it, our author's rule fails, that *whensoever God makes choice of any person to be supreme ruler* (for I suppose the name king has no spell in it, it is not the title, but the power makes the difference) *he intends that the issue also should have the benefit of it,* since from their coming out of *Egypt* to *David*'s time, 400 years, the *issue* was never *so sufficiently comprehended in the person of the father,* as that any son, after the death of his father, succeeded to the government amongst all those judges that judged *Israel.* If, to avoid this, it be said, God always chose the person of the successor, and so, transferring the *fatherly authority* to him, excluded his issue from succeeding to it, that is manifestly not so in the story of *Jephtha,* where he articled with the people, and they made him judge over them, as is plain, *Judg.* 11.

§. 164. It is in vain then to say, that *whensoever God chooses any special person* to have the exercise of *paternal authority,* (for if that be not to be king, I desire to know the difference between a king and one having the exercise of *paternal authority) he intends the issue also should have the benefit of it,* since we find the authority, the judges had, ended with them, and descended not to their *issue;* and if the judges had not *paternal authority,* I fear it will trouble our author, or any of the friends to his principles, to tell who had then the *paternal authority,* that is, the government and supreme power amongst the *Israelites;* and I suspect they must confess that the chosen people of God continued a people several hundreds of years, without any knowledge or thought of this *paternal authority,* or any appearance of monarchical government at all.

§. 165. To be satisfied of this, he need but read the story of the *Levite,* and the war thereupon with the *Benjamites,* in the three last *chapters* of *Judges;* and when he finds, that the *Levite* appeals to the people for justice that it was the tribes and the congregation, that debated, resolved, and directed all that was done on that occasion; he must conclude, either that *God* was not *careful to preserve the fatherly authority* amongst his own chosen people; or else that the *fatherly authority* may be preserved, where there is no monarchical government: if the latter, then it will follow, that though *fatherly authority* be never so well proved, yet it will not infer a necessity of monarchical government; if the former, it will seem very strange and improbable, that God should ordain *fatherly authority* to be so sacred amongst the sons of men, that there could be no power, or government without it, and yet that amongst his own people, even whilst he is providing a government for them, and therein prescribes rules to the several states and relations of men, this great and fundamental one, this most material and necessary of all the rest, should be concealed, and lie neglected for 400 years after.

§. 166. Before I leave this, I must ask how our author knows that *whensoever God makes choice of any special person to be king, he intends that the issue should have the benefit thereof?* Does God by the law of nature or revelation say so? By the same law also he must say, which of his *issue* must enjoy the crown in succession, and so point out the heir, or else leave his *issue* to divide or scramble for the government: both alike absurd, and such as will destroy the benefit of such grant to the *issue.* When any such declaration of God's intention is produced, it will be our duty to believe God intends it so; but till that be done, our author must shew us some better warrant, before we shall be obliged to receive him as the authentic revealer of God's intentions.

§. 167. *The issue,* says our author, *is comprehended sufficiently in the person of the father, although the father only was named in the grant:* and yet God, when he gave the land of *Canaan* to *Abraham, Gen.* xiii. 15. thought fit to put *his seed* into the grant too: so the priesthood was given to *Aaron and his seed;* and the crown God gave not only to *David,* but *his seed* also: and however our author assures us that *God intends, that the issue should have the benefit of it, when he chooses any person to be king,* yet we see that the kingdom which he gave to *Saul,* without mentioning his seed after him, never came to any of his *issue:* and why, when God chose a person to be king, he should intend, that his *issue* should have the benefit of it, more than when he chose one to be judge in *Israel,* I would fain know a reason; or why does a grant of *fatherly authority* to a king more comprehend the *issue,* than when a like grant is made to a judge? Is *paternal authority* by right to descend to the *issue* of one, and not of the other? There will need some reason to be shewn of this difference, more than the name, when the thing given is the same *fatherly authority,* and the manner of giving it, God's choice of the person, the same too; for I suppose our author, when he says, *Godraised up judges,* will by no means allow, they were chosen by the people.

§. 168. But since our author has so confidently assured us of the care of God to preserve the *fatherhood,* and pretends to build all he says upon the authority of the scripture, we may well expect that that people, whose law, constitution and history is chiefly contained in the scripture, should furnish him with the clearest instances of God's care of preserving the fatherly authority, in that people who it is agreed he had a most peculiar care of. Let us see then what state this *paternal authority* or government was in amongst the *Jews,* from their beginning to be a people. It was omitted, by our author's confession, from their coming into *Egypt,* till their return out of that bondage, above 200 years: from thence till God gave the *Israelites* a king, about 400 years more, our author gives but a very slender account of it; nor indeed all that time are there the least footsteps of paternal or regal government amongst them. But then says our author, *God re-established the ancient and prime right of lineal succession to paternal government.*

§. 169. What a *lineal succession to paternal government* was then established, we have already seen. I only now consider how long this lasted, and that was to their captivity, about 500 years: from thence to their destruction by the *Romans,* above 650 years after, the *ancient and prime right of lineal succession to paternal government* was again lost, and they continued a people in the promised land without it. So that of 1750 years that they were God's peculiar people, they had hereditary kingly government amongst them not one third of the time; and of that time there is not the least footstep of one moment of *paternal government, nor the re-establishment of the ancient and prime right of lineal succession to it,* whether we suppose it to be derived, as from its fountain, from *David, Saul, Abraham,* or, which upon our author's principles is the only true, from *Adam.*